also by heather havrilesky

How to Be a Person in the World

Disaster Preparedness

what if this were enough?

essays

heather havrilesky

doubleday | new york

Several pieces first appeared, in significantly different form, in the following publications:
Aeon: "Awaiting Renewal" • *The Atlantic:* "Haunted Womanhood" (10/16/16); "The Sound of Bravado" (7/29/16) • *The Baffler:* "Delusion at the Gastropub" (6/2016); "Fifty Shades of Late Capitalism" (4/2013). • *The Cut:* "It's Never Been Harder to Be Young" (7/14/16); "Don't Call It Toxic Masculinity. They're Sociopathic Baby-Men" (10/5/17); "The Problem with Marie Kondo's Second Book" (1/8/16); "What Romance Really Means After 10 Years of Marriage" (2/9/16) • *Matter/Medium:* "Burning Down the Mouse" (7/14/15) • *The New York Times:* "'Billions' Delivers a Dose of Charisma to Hedge Fund Titans" • *The New York Times Magazine:* "50 Shades of Mad Men" (6/22/12); "794 Ways in Which *BuzzFeed* Reminds Us of Impending Death" (7/3/14); "How to Be a Pioneer Woman Without Ever Leaving the Couch" (3/16/12); "Magically Resistant to the Ego-Bloating Properties of Hollywood Life" (7/22/11); "Some Girls Are Better Than Others" (4/12/12); "TV's New Wave of Women: Smart, Strong, Borderline Insane" (3/12/13); "Why Are Americans So Fascinated with Extreme Fitness?" (10/14/14) • *Salon:* "How Hoarding Shows Cured My Hoarding" (4/10/10)

Book design by Michael Collica
Jacket photograph: Masterfile
Jacket design by Emily Mahon

Library of Congress Cataloging-in-Publication Data
Names: Havrilesky, Heather, author.
Title: What if this were enough? : essays / by Heather Havrilesky.
Description: First edition. | New York : Doubleday, [2018]
Identifiers: LCCN 2018001398 | ISBN 9780385542883 (hardcover) |
ISBN 9780385542890 (e-book)
Subjects: LCSH: Havrilesky, Heather. | Happiness. | Conduct of life. |
Women—Biography. | LCGFT: Essays.
Classification: LCC BF575.H27 H388 2018 | DDC 152.4/2—dc23
LC record available at https://lccn.loc.gov/2018001398

MANUFACTURED IN THE UNITED STATES OF AMERICA

1 3 5 7 9 10 8 6 4 2

First Edition

For my father

contents

introduction

From the day we are born, the world tells us lies about who
we are, how we should live, and what we should sacrifice to
cross some imaginary finish line to success and happiness.
More powerful than the outright lies we're told, though, are
the subtler, broader poisons of our culture, how we ingest and
metabolize them until they feel like a part of us, yet we still
can't figure out why we're sick.

Some of these poisons lie in the most unexpected places:
among our principles and values, in our private hopes and
dreams, in our fears and anxieties about how we should be living and what we might never achieve, in our long-held notions
of what we do and don't deserve and what we should and
should not accept. Some of these poisons are embedded in the
shared ideals of our culture, with its focus on constant improve-

ment and perpetual forward motion. The rise of digital culture
has exacerbated this problem dramatically. We're now, more
than ever before, bombarded by hidden and overt messages
about our personal worth. In spite of the growing uncertainty
and anxiety of our current moment, we are meant to sidestep
inconvenient emotions and fearlessly conquer the future. The
slightest hesitation dooms us to the ranks of failures and losers. No wonder our capacity for nuance and subtlety has been
lost, as our opinions and ideals increasingly take the shape
of fundamentalist religions. Poetry and art, expansive intel-
lectual discourse, the odd unfiltered moment—these are either
misinterpreted as moral litmus tests or else they're upstaged
by bold claims and extremist rhetoric. The blustery overstate-
ments and exaggerations and lies of talk show hosts, pundits,
social media firebrands, and politicians drown out all attempts
at refinement, restraint, and grace, and seep into our everyday
interactions. Thoughtfulness is misread as uncertainty; melancholy is misunderstood as a stubborn refusal to play nicely
with others. A century ago, survival was the main event. Longing was an accepted part of existence. Today, the inability to
achieve happiness or fit in with the herd is treated as a kind of
moral failure.

This book represents my attempt to investigate some of our
most powerful cultural delusions and false dichotomies, to
examine the inaccurate value judgments we make about mundane human behaviors, and to question the continued glorification of suffering, dishonesty, romantic fantasy, conquest,
predation, perfectionism, denial, naïveté, and self-abnegation.
Each essay in this book reflects an effort to examine the odd,
contradictory messages we've slowly internalized without
knowing it. Only by recognizing the absurdity of our guiding assumptions can we cultivate a more organic, enthusiastic,
complex relationship to our lived experience.

Because the state of cultural confusion we're experiencing is anything but trivial. Day in and day out, through aspirational products and heartfelt-seeming commercial messages, in the psychobabble of gurus and the motivational rhythms of Facebook testimonies, between the lines of pop songs and the dialogue of TV comedies, we are taught to communicate triumph while privately experiencing ourselves as inadequate and our lives as disappointing. Instead of recognizing these ingested messages as toxic, we learn to treat our humanity itself as poisonous, to treat our most human desires as a kind of sickness that can only be cured with outside help. Our self-respect, our pride, and our anger are encountered as personal failings, signs of how far off the path of empowerment and enlightenment we've strayed. Day by day, minute by minute, we are robbed of the present.

Which is an odd state of affairs, considering that we're living in a time of unprecedented comfort, leisure, and wealth—albeit one to which only a segment of the population has full access. But few of us are spared the peculiar pressures and anxiety of our current moment. Through the devices in our pockets, we are reminded of our limitless freedom, limitless opportunities, limitless ways to indulge our interests. And yet, our lives feel more difficult to navigate than ever.

Many of the hurdles we face are not concrete and are therefore difficult to address directly. We interact in a world curated mostly by commercial forces. We are pulled into a strange, manic, overcrowded realm of technology that taxes our focus. "What should I be doing right now?" is a question that feels more urgent than ever. Face-to-face, real-time connection to others feels fraught and awkward compared to the safe distance of digital communication. We maintain intimate virtual contact with strangers but seem increasingly isolated from our closest friends and family members.

Our culture exerts a constant pressure on us that severs our relationship to ourselves and each other. This book explores discrete examples of the sources of this severing, along with sweeping views of the larger landscape against which these changes play out. But I also hope to express how it feels to be inside of the problem, to feel these cultural poisons sinking into your skin without always knowing how to keep them out—or even knowing which side effects are attributable to outside forces and which are manifestations of your biochemical quirks, your lopsided personality, your fractured emotional development.

The point of this book is not to drily assess the damage and then step away. Because the maladies I'm describing feel personal to each of us. So many of us share the same symptoms, but we experience them as private and embarrassing. That's part of their insidious hold on us. We need multiple, simultaneous entry points, both to diagnose where we are and to address where we might go from here.

The world takes no responsibility for the sicknesses it incites in us. We are told repeatedly that our destiny is in our hands. We are fed the illusion of self-determination, day after day, then treated as insufficient when we don't overcome the formidable forces working against us.

Our compassion for ourselves and for others remains underdeveloped. We are secluded inside our individual illusions and purchased fairy tales. When we finally realize that not only can't we live our "best" lives, but the entire system is rigged against us, there is no consolation. "Do better," some will say, stepping back and shrugging when confronted with a person in need, or a problem with no easy solution. Without help or understanding from others, it often feels like we have no option but to retreat back into fantasy, in order to reclaim a sense of control.

Our addiction to fantasy and control also leads us to seek a moral for every negative outcome: He got cancer because he held on to his anger. She got rich because she persevered over adversity. He became homeless because he lost faith in his dreams. She became famous because she believed in her passions, against all odds. Hindsight fleshes out the missing pieces in the story, fills in the gaps, checks the box next to the appropriate lesson.

But one moral supersedes all others: When things go wrong, we only have ourselves to blame.

No wonder so many people who write in to my weekly advice column seeking guidance are afraid to choose a path forward and commit to it. They recognize that there's not much support or understanding in store for those who hesitate, change their minds, falter, or flatly reject the widely accepted signifiers of success and happiness. Yet it's rare that we take a step back from our current bewildering moment and observe that many of the things we most passionately embrace are also almost uniformly bad for us.

At a time when our freedom is increasingly threatened by the spread of fascism, the growing gap between the rich and poor, and the ravages of climate change, it might behoove us to analyze just how broken our culture has become and just how poorly it serves us. This might be a good moment to examine how our shared hallucinations and false narratives rob us of our imagination and our humanity, crush our sense of community and our connections to each other, and mute our sympathies for those who are vulnerable or oppressed, while heightening our affection for those who shamelessly oppress and harm others. Because the confusion we now face springs, at least in part, from the purposeful blurring of lines between investigation and propaganda, between facts and entertainment, between fantasy and reality. Having been raised on simple, emotionally reassuring answers to every question, we are made anxious by any attempt to take a critical look at the complex forces at play in the world.

We have a lot of work to do. We have to fight for this world, but we also have to fight for our ability to experience this world more fully. We have to rediscover how to navigate each day. We have to learn how to embrace the imperfection of the present moment and accept the wide range of experiences that fall between happiness and sadness, success and failure, true love and hatred, popularity and invisibility. But in order to do that, we have to examine and deconstruct the reductive solutions and the magical thinking that we've been fed since birth.

More than anything else, we have to imagine a different kind of life, a different way of living. We have to reject the shiny, shallow future that will never come, and locate ourselves in the current, flawed moment. Despite what we've been taught, we are neither eternally blessed nor eternally damned. We are blessed and damned and everything in between. Instead of toggling between victory and defeat, we have to learn to live in the middle, in the gray area, where a real life can unfold on its own time. We have to breathe in reality instead of distracting ourselves around the clock. We have to open our eyes and our hearts to each other. We have to connect with what already is, who we already are, what we already have.

We want too much. We don't need that much to be happy. We can change ourselves, and our world, in part by returning to that simple truth, repeatedly. We have to imagine finally feeling satisfied.

what if this were enough?

the smile factory

The enforced cheer of American life never leaves you alone. From your first day on Earth, you are prodded and provoked with smiling plush toys and grinning mobiles and cloyingly sweet songs that insist on your consistent, unending happiness. Adults point cameras at you until your face grimaces, then produce photos of expressions mostly induced by gas pains. Day in and day out, you are pestered by Barney the Dinosaur, singing about how much everyone loves everyone else and demanding that you turn your frown upside down, in a voice so drippily emphatic that you might like to fashion a shiv out of your sippy cup and gut that purple menace where he stands. But soon, Mickey Mouse and Ronald McDonald and Olaf the Snowman and Tinkerbell add their own urgent yet upbeat demands: Dance! Clap your hands! Believe in magic!

Eat a Happy Meal! Life is a victory march, and only a grouch would steadfastly refuse to join in the fun. What do you have against joy, anyway?

Which is probably fine for babies. What's odd about American culture—and now pop culture at large—is how fervently it insists on keeping us all in a frothy state of upbeat enthusiasm and childlike wonder for the entire stretch of our lives, from birth to death. Even after we mature into adults, even after we experience heartbreak and nagging doubts and disappointments untold, life is still supposed to be dominated by sunshine and big hugs and warm smiles, lathered up into a bubbly storm of upbeat nothingness. Everything must be improving. If things are bad, they are always about to get better. Reluctance to see it that way will be encountered as willful misery. You must be living life to its fullest, always. Even when you are suffering, you are learning important lessons. You are making memories. You are doing this for the experience, which is irreplaceable. Every day is a gift. You are not permitted to sigh deeply, or roll your eyes, or linger skeptically on the sidelines. You are not allowed a little space to be lukewarm, or resigned, or judgmental, or exhausted. Sadness is weak. If you're feeling bad, you must be making bad choices. It's time to make better ones.

Yet this chirpy insistence on positivity has a strange way of enhancing the dread and anxiety and melancholy that lie just beneath the surface of things: your mother's downturned mouth as the phone rings, that strain in your father's voice as he talks about a far-off war, the rain beat on the roof a steady reminder of shadow worlds you don't understand yet. Meanwhile, some sleight of hand makes the bad guys vanish, some secret force keeps the poor and the murderous at bay and prevents the people who get the spare change from your Unicef box from busting down the door to demand your whole piggy bank, your whole house, your whole town.

"Smiles, everyone! Smiles!" Mr. Roarke demands at the start of *Fantasy Island,* that quintessential 1980s bastion of mandatory American cheer. Even though Mr. Roarke's flavor of happiness lives on a mysterious island and has a fruity drink with an umbrella in its hands at all times, that sound of being urged to smile has a familiar echo to it. We are all—in our public lives, in our professional lives, and even in our personal lives—urged to grin along obediently like contestants on *The Bachelor,* hoping against hope that we win some mysterious, coveted prize that we can't see clearly. Smiling along like you're already happy is what leads you to your own Happily Ever After. Refusing to smile, refusing to agree, refusing to comply: These things mean that you are difficult and you want to be unhappy. These things mean that you will make trouble for everyone. These things mean that you will lose and keep losing.

Even as an adult, even as an emancipated, free, independent breadwinner, the enforced cheer of American life is never far away. It's the boss who wants you to be more polite in your email messages, and not point out the obvious sloppy work and bizarre groupthink and passive-aggressiveness and corner-cutting madness that unfold every day without comment. It's the intolerably pushy acquaintance at the party, urging you: drink more, don't worry be happy, don't overthink it, it's all good, stop bumming everyone out. It's the mom at school who wonders aloud why you would choose to "get so heavy" about the news instead of just focusing on "positive things." It's the neighbor who smiles a strained smile and says nothing when you mention that your roof is leaking but you can't afford to fix it yet so you've got a tarp on there until you can. It's always better not to mention the truth, his pained smile tells you. It's always better not to point out that things might get worse before they get better.

In other centuries (and in other lands), melancholy and longing were considered a natural part of the human condition. Now they are a moral failing, a way of signaling to the world that you're a loser and a quitter. You have to change your attitude and play nicely with others, even if that means bullshitting your way through every interaction. Everyone wants to see you turn that frown upside down. Smiles, everyone, smiles! Like you mean it this time.

——

Sometimes I forget that I'm going to die someday, and then *BuzzFeed* reminds me that death is inescapable. Because in its frenzied onslaught of yellow "LOL"s and "fail"s and "10 Dogs Who Went as a Different Dog for Halloween" lies an existential evasion so strained that it can't help inadvertently evoking the specter of mortality. The site may have evolved in recent years, blending serious reporting and somber commentary with lighter fare, but its initial, effortlessly whimsical tone, its habit of sugarcoating longer, heavier reported pieces with deceptively chipper headlines, and its compulsion to quantify and classify everything under the sun once represented the apotheosis of American trivia-focused escapism, served up with an overabundant garnish of "trashy" and "cute" and "yaaass."

This explains the feeling of vertigo that a visit to *BuzzFeed* sometimes induces: the sense that the world is spinning faster and faster, every inch of virgin land filling to its borders with "34 People You Probably Didn't Know Were on *Seinfeld*" and "24 Super Cute Drawings of Fashionable Celebrities" and "21 Snoozing Koalas You Want to Snuggle With Right Now."

The editors of *BuzzFeed* recognized a long time ago that

successful diversion depended on continually toggling its joystick between micronostalgia for the past ("55 Things Only '90s Teenage Girls Can Understand") and microexaminations of the latest microtrend ("The 'Gingers Have Souls' Kid Just Released a Hip-Hop Music Video"). *BuzzFeed* could simultaneously pretend that joy was an ever-renewable resource ("13 Cute Kid Vines You'll Watch Over and Over Again") while also hinting that our stores of happiness were dangerously low and dwindling ("13 Holidays You've Been Celebrating Totally Wrong").

BuzzFeed so typified a mode of social engagement common to the early 2010s that it inspired *The Onion* to spin off a parody site called *ClickHole* in 2014. Where *The Onion* once lampooned the "area man" argot of local newspapers, *ClickHole* spoofs the relentless exuberance of *BuzzFeed*'s nonsensical hierarchies and shrieking enticements. But *ClickHole*, in spite of its appropriately abyss-conjuring name, can only touch the hem of *BuzzFeed*'s bizarre signature house style. (*ClickHole*: "16 Pictures of Beyoncé Where She's Not Sinking in Quicksand.") So far, it never fully captures the self-parodying brilliance of the real thing. (*BuzzFeed*: "22 Celebrities That Look Nothing Alike.")

And the more time you spend on *BuzzFeed*, the more the boundaries between "win" and "fail" seem to blur. After a while, it's impossible not to slip into a dissociative trance, in which you surrender to the allure of a perpetual, trivial nowhereland, nestled somewhere between "15 Cats That You Don't Want to Mess With" and "44 Hong Kong Movie Subtitles Gone Wrong."

The past is reduced to a slide show. The future is a YouTube video that won't load. And the present is a jumble of jaunty yellow buttons blurting "omg" and "awww" and "tl;dr." What else can we do but click through?

BuzzFeed's eternal, upbeat present tense exemplifies the frenetic pressures of our current screen-driven moment. Ironically, though, by reinforcing the supremacy of rapidly expiring distractions, the site often incites the feeling that you might be wasting your time on old news. In every "Tell Us Your Zodiac Sign and We'll Tell You What Alcoholic Beverage You Are" and "17 Pictures That Should Be Considered Crimes Against Humanity," the site privileges the current moment above all others. But this tireless fixation on novelty now feels familiar and therefore also dated. When BuzzFeed headlines blur into each other, they start to smell like 2011. Isn't there somewhere else we're supposed to be?

Its status as prematurely aging novelty makes *BuzzFeed* the ultimate petri dish in which the queasy mood of the current moment is replicated. No wonder it incites such restless feelings of dread; its repeating message couldn't be clearer: You are not happy enough. This is not good enough. You need bigger, better, brighter distractions. You need newer flashy "wtf"s and "omg"s. You are running out of time.

—

This unnervingly chirpy, rapidly expiring present certainly wasn't invented by *BuzzFeed*. It arose as part of a long tradition of manic enthusiasm that can be traced, at least in part, to the dawn of radio—the first popular medium that combined advertising jingles and patriotic slogans and Judeo-Christian optimism into a distinctly American soundtrack of mandatory cheer.

I still remember the sinking sensation I felt as a kid the first time I heard a radio D.J. rave about something called a "Toyotathon." It was the summer after my parents' divorce, which my mother kept assuring me was all for the best. That might explain why listening to someone trying to persuade me that a car sale is just like an all-night carnival struck me as just another example of the kind of blatant emotional trickery with which I was newly acquainted.

Soon, the continual stream of pop music and chipper ads that flowed from the radio seemed to form an extended cacophonous jingle of denial, and the incessant clamor of A&W Root Beer ads and *Magnum, P.I.* opening credits and Hall & Oates songs and ads for Sizzlin' Summer Sales incited within me a pure blast of sadness. The "Yum, Yum, Bumble Bee, Bumble Bee Tuna" song; the hyperactive leprechaun searching for his Frosted Lucky Charms; the assurance that "Nothing beats a great pair of L'eggs!" had all begun to trigger a haunting sense in me that life could never be as happy and exciting as it pretended to be on TV and the radio. Casey Kasem's lilting, sentimental speech patterns on *American Top 40* started to sound like another form of the catechism we repeated at my Catholic church every Sunday.

Death and disappointment were suddenly everywhere—in the news every night, at the breakfast table in the morning—but rather than acknowledge the burden of such things, we'd all agreed to smile along, taking our cues from Captain Stubing and Captain Kangaroo and Cap'n Crunch. The famous yellow smiley face, that fifty-year-old precursor to *BuzzFeed*'s yellow buttons, urged us to Have a Happy Day, but it sounded to me less like a request than a command.

And today, as the planet heats to a low simmer and ominous images of polar bears swimming in circles make us feel like the universe's most reckless zookeepers, admonishments to embrace optimism and cheer and "greatness" are more vehement than ever. It's as though the gentle reggae strains of Bobby McFerrin's "Don't Worry, Be Happy" have been sped up to a ska beat, and both worrying and unhappiness are now treated not just as a taboo but as an affliction you have a responsibility to treat. Curmudgeonly remarks, high-strung habits, and skepticism once merely meant you were a certain type of person, negative but relatively harmless, like Oscar the Grouch from *Sesame Street*. But these days, "grouchiness" is often encountered as a condition for which you require intervention: a prescription, more meditation, more self-care, a subscription to *O, The Oprah Magazine*.

Even as depression and anxiety, or else simple dissatisfaction with the state of things, are as prevalent as ever, we are urged to get over these feelings, to recover from them, to bounce back quickly, or else to conceal them. To do otherwise is to embrace the "fail." You are not following the rules. Start acting like a happy winner or you might become a depressed loser forever.

—

The summer after my parents got divorced and my dad moved out of our house, I happened to pick up John Updike's *Rabbit Is Rich*. It was the first novel that felt real and relatable to me, like being injected straight into the bloodstream of another human being. And no wonder—Updike knew exactly how the intrusions of pop-culture minutiae had the power to evoke the cheery dread of Middle America.

Updike's protagonist, Rabbit Angstrom, is a former high school basketball star who feels hemmed in by the American dream—cornered by his alcoholic wife, Janice, and upstaged by his ineffectual, self-pitying son, Nelson. And every step of the way, Rabbit experiences his entrapment and impending death through the lens of pop trivia, snippets of experience Updike once referred to as "giv[ing] the mundane its beautiful due."

As a result, the Rabbit tetralogy offers a slow-motion glimpse at the rise of mass culture over the course of three decades. In *Rabbit, Run* (1960), Rabbit's argument with his wife is punctuated by Mouseketeer musical numbers and Tootsie Roll ads. As he drives out of his hometown to escape his crumbling marriage, he's lulled by commercials for Rayco Clear Plastic Seat Covers and New Formula Barbasol Presto-Lather. In *Rabbit Redux* (1971), news that Janice might be cheating on Rabbit is interspersed with scenes from a nearby TV, where "people are trying to guess what sort of prize is hidden behind a curtain and jump and squeal and kiss each other when it turns out to be an eight-foot frozen-food locker."

By *Rabbit Is Rich* (1981), Updike's protagonist enters a kind of pop-culture fugue state, in which a ghastly pastiche of gas lines and Chuck Wagon restaurants and Skylab mishaps and Donna Summer's "Hot Stuff" on the radio blends seamlessly with his sentimentality and boredom and inescapable fear of death. Rabbit worries that "tomorrow will be the same as yesterday," and in the background, his mother-in-law's television blares the latest news of the Iran hostage crisis. The noisy trivia that surrounds Rabbit, with its eternal present-tense merriment, feels increasingly oppressive: "The world keeps ending but new people too dumb to know it keep showing up as if the fun's just started."

Finally, in *Rabbit at Rest* (1990), cultural tidbits start to take on the same indistinct shape as his own life's events: "Like everything else on the news, you get bored, disasters get to seem a gimmick, like all those TV tuneouts in football." As hard as Rabbit tries to beat back his dread with the "win" signifiers of his era—wealth, an affair, a few chummy but superficial friendships, an uneven golf game—none of Rabbit's fixes last. His powerlessness, his rampant sexual urges, his unrelenting nostalgia for his own lonely past are encapsulated and eventually superseded by a steady flow of trivial distractions. That moment in the novel when a leap of a man into the air on a Toyota commercial ("Oh, what a feeling!") yields to the cold air above Lockerbie, where Pan Am Flight 103 exploded in 1988, demonstrates exactly how the enthusiasms of American life thinly mask the specter of death. When Rabbit unceremoniously falls dead of a heart attack, it's clear that this is how most stories will end. Even as he lies dying, his son insists on Frosted Flakes over bran cereals, and the newspaper arrives, blaring "Hugo Clobbers South Carolina."

Five years after *Rabbit at Rest* was published, my own father died of an unexpected heart attack. The day after that, Pete Sampras beat Andre Agassi in the finals of the U.S. Open. "You Are Not Alone" by Michael Jackson was the No. 1 song on the radio. Orville Redenbacher died of a heart attack nine days later. Thirteen days after that, O. J. Simpson was proclaimed not guilty by a jury in Los Angeles. The latest news, whether upbeat or ominous, was reported in the same manic, excitable tone, one that was utterly out of sync with my dark emotional state. Sadness is a lonely thing in America. Taking time to reflect means acknowledging that you were once sad, or that you lost something along the way that you might never get back.

—

When everything is bent into a jolly shape, everything feels more mournful than it should. This is how the hopeful words of wisdom inscribed on a tea bag slowly take on the weight of an omen, and the funeral dirge and the bubbly pop anthem eventually start to sound like the same song. In its abhorrence of mixed feelings, American pop culture incites mixed feelings, every step of the way. No wonder canny filmmakers and TV producers like Steven Spielberg and Matthew Weiner inserted the ambient glee of Saturday-morning cartoons and radio D.J.s gushing about the weather in order to conjure foreboding and suspense in their work. It's the same kind of suspense that sets in when you spend too much time on *BuzzFeed* and its ilk, that manic cheeriness-at-gunpoint feeling representing a pure distillation of the American mood. There are no buttons for "sad!" or "dark" or "melancholy."

Updike captured the precise ways that our culture kicks up so much private ambivalence and regret without offering a salve for these feelings. But he also illustrated what we stand to lose when we mask our dread with peanut brittle and daiquiris and "If I Didn't Care" by Connie Francis. Rabbit Angstrom sought salvation from his domestic and spiritual trap, but he never achieved it. He knew there was more to life; he just couldn't find it. And every time he tried to look for it, everyone around him treated him like he was being selfish, or stubborn, or hopelessly uncooperative.

It's no wonder that, when Nelson urged him not to die, Rabbit responded with a single word: "Enough."

the happiest place on earth

No matter how your heart is grieving over the absurd cost, Disneyland has become a kind of mandatory pilgrimage for parents of young children. But even after you navigate the labyrinthine parking structure and slog amid impossible crowds pushing double-wide strollers across miles of hot concrete, even after you stand in the last of a dozen endless lines, all the while fielding existential riddles from your kids like "Why are we *still* standing here?" and "What are we *doing*?," even after you endure a series of lackluster rides that amount to interactive advertisements for undead franchises, no sense of calm and well-being descends. You don't feel proud of yourself for delivering the dream of Disney to your offspring. Instead, you feel like you've yanked your impressionable kids straight into the tyrannically cheerful cult of consumerist culture. As George Clooney's character tells a young optimist at the start of Disney's *Tomorrowland,* "You've been manipulated into thinking you were part of something incredible. You thought you were special, but you're not."

But your skepticism—like his—is just a setup for that climactic moment when old-fashioned, Disney-style hope wins out. Nearly religious positivity in the face of doom lies at the heart of the Disney brand, after all—which may be why Banksy's Dismaland, a theme-park homage to dystopian despair that operated in the British seaside town of Weston-super-Mare for a few months in 2015, could incite such a powerful feeling of vertigo. The street artist couldn't have had better timing: Somehow a company built around a cartoon mouse has miraculously evolved and expanded and weathered countless storms of widespread skepticism, not to mention jacked-up ticket prices, overcrowding, and a measles outbreak in 2014 that didn't conjure fantasy or frontier or future so much as the perils of life in South Sudan. Along with the huge chunk of cultural mindshare in its pocket (ESPN, ABC, the Disney Channel, *Star Wars,* Pixar, Marvel), Disney has amassed thousands of sprawling acres of immaculate, branded property worldwide, from Disneyland Paris to Tokyo Disneyland to Hong Kong Disneyland, every foot of it haunted by the triumphant strains of "Once Upon a Dream" or "Bibbidi-Bobbidi-Boo" emitting from omnipresent speakers, every sight and sound and sensation a carefully honed feat of interactive advertising that continues to draw in toddlers and teenagers and singles and couples and victorious athletes and dying children alike.

This is exactly the fairy tale that Banksy aimed to disrupt with Dismaland, bleak but unforgettable in its filthy, crumbling concrete spaces, its depressed park attendants clad in mouse ears, its orca emerging from a toilet, its boats full of immigrants circling ghost-faced through a polluted pond. Such images may be simplistic, but they're meant to hit us at the same simple level that Disneyland itself does. While Cinderella's corpse hanging from a toppled carriage as paparazzi cameras flash might strike some onlookers as overly obvious, it's obvious by design. The catastrophes unfolding around us aren't hard to miss, after all, but we continue to avert our eyes. As our public spaces worldwide are transformed into matching, carefully designed corporate realms dominated by shiny, flashing screens, the filth of Dismaland feels like the foreshock of looming disaster. Or maybe we're just being confronted by the disasters that have already started to engulf our world, so omnipresent that no flock of singing birds or merry pirates can distract us any longer. But more than toppled carriages or angry Mouseketeers, it's the filth of Dismaland that unnerves us the most. This is the reality of suffering that we work so hard to avoid.

This avoidance of grime and discomfort was exactly what Walt Disney had in mind when he dreamed up Disneyland. He wanted to provide a nostalgic passage to small-town America in a time of anxiety, and to embody the adventurous, can-do spirit of the country, back when Americans still believed in its Gilded Age destiny as a city upon a hill, a shining example of liberty and prosperity for the rest of the world to emulate. That notion has long since expired, of course. As J. G. Ballard put it in 1983, the American dream "no longer supplies the world with its images, its dreams, its fantasies . . . It supplies the world with its nightmares now."

In Disneyland, we recognize the outlines of how privileged America has protected itself from harsh reality for decades, and the ways that some of us have come to prefer these protections, this fakeness, to reality itself. Where as recently as the 1970s many of us decried mass-produced entertainment and the stultifying sameness of corporate-owned spaces, by the 2000s we

were humming anthems from *Frozen* and forsaking relatively
lackluster public parks for the much more engrossing modern
playground of the Apple Store. Today, even the quirkiest corners of the internet are crowded with full-color, interactive ads
for the last corporate commodity we searched for on Amazon
or mentioned in passing on Facebook, and now those random
searches will result in phone calls from telemarketers who
seem to know more about us than we know about ourselves.

But no matter how we try to wriggle into some virgin corner
of the world free from screens or cameras or phones, unsullied
by flashing ads or surveillance, devoid of jubilant ballads or
beeping devices, we fail. We're all plugged into a shiny, down-
home, buoyant, authentic-seeming global simulacrum, one
that not only doesn't belong to us, but bleeds us of our sanity,
our money, and our privacy and sells them off to the highest
bidder. Not surprisingly, the commercialized fantasy of American life has only rendered us more ravenous and impossible
to satisfy. The illusory corporate grid of fanciful characters is
real; we are the imaginary ones. The Disneyfication of culture
is complete.

—

When my kids started clamoring to go to Disneyland around
ages six and eight (it had been three years since they first visited as very young children), their anticipation was propor-
tionate to my dread. I dreaded Disneyland with every cell of
my being. It wasn't the crowds or the lines or the avalanche
of overpriced plastic. I was anxious about the micro-horrors
of Disney, those little visions that can plunge you into a
state of existential despair: greasy femur-sized turkey legs
being ripped off the bone by adults in Minnie Mouse ears;
struggling actors dressed as Mary Poppins and Bert, improvis-

ing cheerful chatter in fake British accents; husky children in *Tangled* T-shirts burying their faces in giant clouds of cotton candy in the Mad Tea Party teacup ride line, then vomiting down the sides of trash cans afterward; the teal and purple eyeshadow of Ariel, which inevitably calls to mind the signature style of certain members of the mid-1990s Russian Olympic figure skating team.

Somehow, the little things—the eavesdropped-on conversations, the tense family dynamics—take on a special kind of heaviness when you're visiting Disneyland. As Joseph Conrad put it in *Heart of Darkness,* "They had behind them, to my mind, the terrific suggestiveness of words heard in dreams, of phrases spoken in nightmares." The semi-hypnotic state of helplessness you enter is central to the experience of Disney. All of your membranes become porous; the sadness can enter your bloodstream directly. You are removed from all familiar signifiers, and it makes you all the more vulnerable. You are trying to be a good parent, but there you are, defenseless, in a vast sea of human beings, huddled in their desperate gaggles, squabbling, regretful, sweating profusely, scarfing Mickey Mouse–shaped beignets and cups of frozen lemonade and hot dogs bathed in oily chili, all of them simultaneously beating back that inevitable feeling of melancholy that comes from being at The Happiest Place on Earth, and discovering that they're deeply, inescapably unhappy.

I'd been cajoled into a return trip by my younger daughter, who barely remembered her first visit beyond an unnerving spin through a Roger Rabbit–themed nightmare. My stress was mounting, and the newly increased $99 ticket price wasn't helping (tickets were $1 when the park opened in 1955; Disney World tickets were $3.50 when that park opened in 1971). Recognizing that there was no escape from overspending, I behaved in the paradoxical manner of a trapped animal who

suddenly becomes aggressively confrontational: I leaned in—
way in, beyond reason. I went from feeling queasy over the
enormous cost of every single stupid thing on the Disney website to signing up for *all* of the things, the two-day tickets, the
overpriced Disneyland Hotel, the even more overpriced Grand
Californian Hotel & Spa. I made reservations at faux-fancy
Disney restaurants; I noted the times of parades, fireworks,
and the World of Color water show, whatever the hell that
was. I projected myself and my husband and our two daughters into every gauzy photo on the site, all of us smiling and
frolicking like extras in the opening credits to ABC's *Wonderful World of Disney*. No driving there and back in a single day,
getting up in the dark and returning in the dark and negoti-
ating with exhausted kids all day long. "We have to go full
Mickey," I told my skeptical husband. "We can't half-ass it this
time."

Spending more money ensures greater happiness. This is the
confused thinking of the duped consumer. In my deluded state,
a gargantuan price tag meant we would finally see Disney
through the eyes of our California-born, Disneyland-loving
friends, with their pricey yearlong passes and beloved Mickey
Mouse sweatshirts. These friends, half of them childless, visit
Disneyland for birthdays and anniversaries and spontaneous,
no-excuse-at-all midweek day trips. One friend even got married as the nightly fireworks display lit up the sky, the strains
of "A Dream Is a Wish Your Heart Makes" a stand-in for
Pachelbel's Canon in D.

These friends aren't being ironic. They unabashedly love eating Dole Whip in the Enchanted Tiki Room and riding Space
Mountain and touring the Haunted Mansion for the fortieth
time. They love eating cotton candy and cruising on the Mark
Twain Riverboat and rumbling along on Big Thunder Mountain Railroad. They know that the roller coaster derailed in

2003, and they don't care. They view the park as something like inherited land, their beloved Uncle Walt's antiquated but still luxurious estate. Each return trip kicks up soothingly familiar memories of the trips that came before it.

Which is exactly how Walt Disney wanted them to feel. As Neil Gabler points out in *Walt Disney: The Triumph of the American Imagination,* this escapist slant was apparent in the park's promotional brochures. "[W]hen you enter Disneyland, you will find yourself in the land of yesterday, tomorrow, and fantasy," one brochure declared. "Nothing of the present exists in Disneyland." This sense of deliverance is echoed in the voices of the Disneyland lovers I know. "It helped me forget for a few hours that my parents were divorcing," one friend told me, "and helped me cope with the teen angst years. I could enjoy myself like a kid and feel safe in a way that wasn't possible outside of those walls."

Of course, Disneyland was also intended to be an enormous and groundbreaking interactive advertisement for the Walt Disney company, just as ABC's then-new TV show *Disneyland* (an anthology program that had several different titles, most memorably *The Wonderful World of Disney*) and the soon-to-follow *Mickey Mouse Club* were both advertisements for Disneyland. Indeed, Disney himself said: "The main idea of the program is to sell." Pointing out the cross-marketing benefits of the show sounds downright quaint today, when brands are rarely judged on the quality or consistency or purity of their product so much as on their bulletproof, cross-platform international market penetration.

Somehow, this crass reality faded quickly from my mind the moment we set foot on Disneyland property. Because from the first second we arrived, we were treated not like consumers, but like the only humans alive. Considering that an average of 44,000 people visit the park every day, this is a jaw-dropping feat. My daughter was given a "Happy Birthday!" button from the valet when we reached the Disneyland Hotel, and from that point forward, every adult who interacted with us wished her a happy birthday. (As she was unaccustomed to such kindness from total strangers, this only made her suspicious. What do these needy adults in ugly blue vests want from me?)

We entered the park flanked by humans yelping "Happy birthday!" and "Have a magical day!" every few feet. We ate Dole Whip in the Enchanted Tiki Room. We spun through the Pirates of the Caribbean. (Among other updates to the ride, an animatronic pirate who once chased an unfortunate animatronic girl around a house now chased a girl carrying a cake.) We had lunch at the Blue Bayou, a chilly, dimly lit restaurant inside the Pirates of the Caribbean ride. I ordered a Monte Cristo sandwich (basically a ham-and-cheese doughnut) and a mint julep with a fake ice cube that glowed in rapidly shifting rainbow colors. Our lunch may have had the overcooked, oversalted quality of hotel food, but the kids were too excited about the glowing ice cubes to care.

I expected the lines to grow and the kids' moods to deteriorate. But thanks to minimal midweek crowds, lines were no longer than fifteen minutes, and everyone stayed cheerful. Even the crowds around us seemed benevolent instead of grouchy. The children we saw all seemed to be smiling, maybe because most of them were holding some form of sugar or standing in line to meet Cinderella. We made it into Star Tours in ten minutes flat, then whipped through the Mad Tea Party and Mr. Toad's Wild Ride. Next, we dashed through It's a Small World. There was a woman in line for the carousel whose legs were tattooed to look like she was wearing lace-up fishnet hose. They looked less fancy than disfigured, the kind of micro-horror I'd expected to reel from, but for some reason it didn't bother me. There was music everywhere, always surging romantically or bouncing along happily, the soundtrack to the most delightful, exciting, emotionally satisfying day you've had in your entire life.

I didn't even realize I was having a great day—arguably a *magical* day—until later that afternoon. I was standing in the town square of what seemed like an adorable whistle-stop hamlet in Middle America, near a patch of green grass, and I had just been told a parade was about to roll by. Soon the music swelled and a chorus of voices sang, "It's a music celebration, come on come on come on, strike up the band!" Some drummers appeared, grinning and dancing down the street, beating their drums enthusiastically. My daughters had big smiles on their faces. They'd just eaten a gigantic poof of pink and yellow cotton candy and a frozen lemonade. I was sipping a large iced coffee, which might explain why the words "Feel the beat, what a great sensation, come on come on come on, move and clap your hands!" inspired me to start clapping along. My husband, similarly caffeinated, hoisted our younger daughter over his head and started swaying in time to the music. "This is what life is all about," I thought, marveling that I had dreaded this trip just the night before. "Enjoying being alive, together, in the moment, as a family, as a community, even, sharing something positive and celebratory and real, right here and now!"

I looked around at the people in the square—other members of my community! Part of the human family!—expecting to see them smiling and clapping the way we were, if not dancing, cheering, and weepily embracing each other. Instead, they stood motionless, or else sat in chairs or on the curb, taking in the parade as though they were watching it from home. Some were recording video of it. Others squinted at their phones, trying to read texts or emails, or maybe watching something else entirely. A few kids and adults were clapping, but most were standing still, staring at the spectacle rolling by. The drummers and the dancers and Mickey and Minnie appeared to be having some kind of peak experience, but the crowd was a sea of blank faces, as if they weren't there at all.

And like that, the spell was broken. I began to notice the details that had until then escaped my attention. I saw the metal railing that encircled the grass. The grass is for viewing, it suggested, not for touching or playing or lounging on. According to Gabler, Disney imagined "a Main Village with a railroad station and a village green . . . a place for people to sit and rest; mothers and grandmothers can watch over small children at play." This town square was not a village green, I saw now, but a stage set—a gorgeously designed sea of hot cement graced by a smattering of small trees. A few feet away, a man in a blue Disney shirt was scanning the crowd and mumbling into his walkie-talkie. This spontaneous community celebration was a carefully choreographed, rigidly scripted corporate spectacle. My family and I were manipulated into thinking we were part of something incredible. We thought we were special, but we were not.

—

At Disneyland today, participation mostly means standing or sitting and passively staring at whatever is in front of you. Participation requires nothing of the participants. You load your body into the little car or boat. You put on your seat belt. You keep your hands inside the vehicle. You sit on the curb until the parade arrives. You file into the viewing area for the massive World of Color water fountain to spring to life. ("Color, color, color!" a chorus exalts as rainbow colors shoot into the sky; Disney never had much of a taste for subtlety.) When it's done, you clap weakly and file out. You are never asked to move or speak or sing. You are treated like a valuable person, but you're never asked to demonstrate your value. When Ariel or Cinderella or the Mad Hatter appears in Fantasyland or Main Street, U.S.A., they ask a kid's name and then simply hold forth for a minute or so in character before the kid is shuffled off and the next kid is led up to them. We are all here, but we're not here. You can try to take part, speak up, get into it, but the implicit message is that you really shouldn't. You are here to passively absorb the brand, and then buy some stuff that signifies and cements your allegiance on the way out. For all of its analog charms—animatronic birds that trade witty banter, hammy young actors in Disney Prince costumes, primitive Small World dolls shaped by outdated cultural clichés—Disneyland is a real-life, interactive experience in which you're meant to treat everything around you like it's appearing on an IMAX screen.

It shouldn't be surprising that Disney's idealistic dreams would evolve into a passive consumer experience in which the individual feels powerful but has no power at all. The same process is reflected across the corporate sphere: Our most imaginative and thoughtful entrepreneurs create something new, guided by an ideology and values that ring true. Steve Jobs had an evangelistic vision of the personal liberation that technology could bring to our lives ("If you give [people] tools they'll do wonderful things with them"). Mark Zuckerberg was inspired by "helping people to connect" and sought to "create more empathic relationships." Jeff Bezos wanted to "invent" and "innovate" and "put customers first." ("We get to work in the future," he proclaimed in one shareholder report, sounding like a true disciple of Walt Disney.) Jack

Dorsey, cofounder of Twitter, has said that the company was created, in part, to generate more understanding and empathy between citizens of the global community. We take comfort in the belief that these ideals are guiding our business leaders and shaping our culture. We are to understand pioneering and profiteering as compatible goals. When Bezos tells *Business Insider*'s Henry Blodget, "I want to see millions of people living and working in [outer] space," it encourages us to view him as a passionate visionary, not a man whose foremost concern is persuading shareholders of his company's future growth, even if that includes not just putting small bookstores out of business but putting *all* other stores out of business.

The problem with the fairy tale of constant growth and constant expansion—the central drive of all publicly traded ventures—is that companies start off with modest goals and creative business plans and then, by dint of their own success, they're cornered into following the reigning script of high-capitalist world domination, swapping out true, steady innovation for aggressive initiatives and mergers that promise the quickest route to infinity and beyond. "We're branching into everything under the sun!" corporate CEOs announce (in sync with the pop stars and struggling entrepreneurs and freelance jacks-of-all-trades who follow in their footsteps), and the company's original ideals are soon lost in the mix.

For all of their talk of connecting the world and putting customers first, Facebook, Amazon, and Google are effectively in the business of mining our personal data. When we learn that Google View cars were outfitted with software not just for mapping our streets but for stealing data off our personal computers via unsecured Wi-Fi networks, we should feel not just intruded upon but betrayed. In 2015, Amazon's digital display ad revenue outstripped even Google's (which in turn outstripped the ad revenue of all U.S. print magazines and newspapers combined), making them our international Everything Store, to the detriment of countless smaller businesses worldwide. Disney itself is far from immune: Disney World's new MagicBands—rubber wristbands with an RFID chip and a radio inside—are capable of replacing tickets and cash, offering the ease of preordered food at restaurants. But they also track your movements through the park, dutifully surveilling and recording your preferences and desires. It's a small world, after all.

Corporations are the new world leaders, more powerful than most nations and more entitled to willfully ignore the rights of citizens in pursuit of continued dominance by reaping profits that far outstrip the economies of most countries. Disney made $55.63 billion in 2016, an amount that would make it the eighty-second-biggest economy in the world, edging out Uruguay ($54.5 billion) and Lebanon ($51.9 billion). Apple's revenue in 2016, $215.6 billion, would make it the forty-seventh-biggest economy in the world, larger than those of Iceland, Croatia, El Salvador, Jordan, Senegal, and Honduras combined.

Disney follows the reigning corporate playbook of conquistador-like growth in every direction at once. The company's Disney Junior channel hooks kids into the brand before they hit preschool. The acquisition of Marvel and *Star Wars* brings into the Mouse's vast empire two franchises with the iconic significance and feverishly devoted followings of most world religions. A proposed merger with Fox would expand Disney's properties beyond comprehension. And Disney always seems to stay in touch with shifts in public sentiment. When feminists decried the regressive nature of the Disney Princess franchise, Disney answered with *Frozen*'s princesses, who prioritize their sisters over empty romantic promises from princes (but retain the sugary voices, fifteen-inch waists, and giant sparkling gowns of their predecessors, as well as their habits of forsaking unwieldy emotions like rage or ambivalence).

It helps Disney's case that in the last fifteen years we've gone from lamenting our insipid cultural artifacts (action movies, misogynistic pop songs, aggressively stupid sitcoms, transparent publicity stunts) to not just exalting them but also admiring the process of their creation. Being a "great brand" or staying "on-brand" is now a high accolade. Meanwhile, being suspicious of manufactured authenticity and global branding is *itself* suspicious, tantamount to distinguishing between high and low culture (elitist!) or labeling the predictable, dull, or ubiquitous as "basic" (snob!). The very concept of selling out has fallen out of the modern lexicon.

Against this cultural backdrop, it's not hard to understand why Banksy's Dismaland was painted by its critics as naïve, reductive, repetitive, and deeply uncool, another act of ego-driven attention-seeking. Ben Luke of the London *Evening Standard* proclaimed that Banksy's Dismaland was "mostly selfie-friendly stuff, momentarily arresting, quickly forgotten—art as clickbait." Others emphasized its pointlessness. "[I]f Banksy has the money to make an entire theme park, WHY NOT JUST USE IT TO HELP PEOPLE!?" squawked John Trowbridge of *The Huffington Post*. Banksy could "fund a school in Africa" or "make a video encouraging the youth to be positive and engaged." Has there ever been a more Disneyfied vision of what it takes to change the world? Ignore all the bad stuff out there and post a super-inspiring video to YouTube instead.

When Disney CEO Robert A. Iger announced in a May 2015 press release, "[O]ur proven franchise strategy creates long-term value across all of our businesses," he meant that each zombie franchise—*The Little Mermaid, Toy Story, Fro-*

zen, *Pirates of the Caribbean*—encourages us to rewatch those earlier movies, buy more merchandise, return to the parks, bring home artifacts that encourage us to do more of the same. And this formula works: Disney stock hit an all-time high in 2015.

As parents, we resist Disney briefly when our kids are toddlers, but eventually most of us get tired and succumb. There's just too much Disney in the world to fight it, especially when you think of the company less as Robert Iger and his shareholders and more as Mickey Mouse and Indiana Jones and Luke Skywalker. After all these years, Disney still embodies our most dearly held ideals: bravery, honor, and standing up for the underdog. Instead of resistance, we tell ourselves that this must be what happiness feels like: total surrender.

—

On the second day of our visit, we discovered that Disney's California Adventure Park was hot, flat, and crowded. All of the careful design and calming dimensions that made Disneyland feel like a safe, soothing escape from the present were gone, supplanted by loud noises, whizzing gears, and unbroken stretches of pavement that heat up unbearably in the midday sun. After hours of wandering through this maze of shadeless, charmless "amusements," from the absurdly ugly pink and gray Tower of Terror to the overheated, gasoline-fumed Radiator Springs Racers, our Disney dream was rapidly curdling into a nightmare. So my family and I sought refuge in the dark, air-conditioned theater of *It's Tough to Be a Bug!*, which promised kid-focused amusement. There were warnings about big bugs and loud sounds, but come on, how frightening could fake bugs be?

Pretty damn frightening, as it turned out. The show was

a blaring, banging gauntlet of surprises designed to scare the living daylights out of the audience, from the animated bugs onscreen who shouted every line to the giant stuffed spiders that dropped from the ceiling and dangled just above our heads, causing both of my daughters to cry softly and shield their eyes with their hands. And just when we thought it was over, a wall in the theater appeared to crumble to the ground with a thundering crash and a giant animatronic grasshopper— Hopper, the tyrannical antagonist of *A Bug's Life*—bellowed menacingly at the audience. The moment embodied everything Disneyland was never supposed to be: loud, jarring, dirty, and unsafe.

In that air-conditioned theater, the existential despair I'd been dreading finally arrived, but it wasn't the micro-horrors of consumerism that brought me there. It was the sudden sense that Disneyland gives us such a clear and disturbing snapshot of where we've landed as a culture. We have collectively sur-rendered all personal agency and control for the sake of a safe, smooth fantasy. Yet in spite of our efforts, here we are living in a world that's louder, more jarring, and far more danger-ous than we had ever anticipated. Corporate escapism can't insulate us from the ugliness of reality anymore. We've been ushered, docile as sheep, into a future that's far from the one we'd imagined. And now we're left staring at each other in disbelief, asking, "How did we get here? Who stood back and let this happen to our world?"

Long after the menacing grasshopper goes silent, a terrified toddler in the row ahead of us kept screaming at the top of his lungs. "Don't worry, it's not real," his father told him, but the boy didn't believe him.

to infinity and beyond

Y ou can have one girlfriend or three," my father once
told me, "but never two. When two girlfriends find
out about each other, you've got trouble." Presumably
two girlfriends would gouge each other's eyes out, whereas
three girlfriends might unpack a picnic lunch of tea sandwiches and cherry wine, lovingly braid each other's hair, and
then fall asleep in the sun together.

Just as my father always offered advice that only applied to
him (he was recently divorced at the time and had embarked
on a lifestyle of juggling as many girlfriends as possible), his
approach to such matters was usually more sporting than practical. I often suspected that he viewed dating several women
at once (while making sure they never found out about each
other) as a worthy goal in part because it was such a difficult

one. Even when he appeared to have more than he could handle, he was always on the lookout for fresh intrigue. But any suggestion that he might marry one of his girlfriends was met with an incredulous laugh, followed by a dour look. "Playing house is hell," he would murmur darkly, as if the entire history of monogamous love were an elaborate game of make-believe.

His alternative to domestic imprisonment seemed to be a never-ending parade of new women: tall and short, blonde and brunette, young and younger. At one point, there was a Big Debbie, a Little Debbie, and a Lawyer Debbie. What could be less pragmatic than three girlfriends with the same name, one of them skilled in the art of argument? But more than convenience or variety, my dad seemed to savor the vision of himself that endless choices implied: He was the master of his own carnal fate, surrounded by an embarrassment of riches.

Although such insatiable conquistador habits might sound borderline sociopathic, his approach to sexual conquest made a kind of twisted sense in the 1980s and '90s, the glory days of his divorced bachelorhood. An economist who'd long since abandoned Marx for Milton Friedman, he was prone to quoting Gordon Gekko from *Wall Street* in a tone that implied that the maxim "Greed is good" was less a self-serving excuse than an expression of one of his core values, one that naturally should extend outside the realm of finance.

His real message, as I saw it, was this: The world and everything in it is yours for the taking. Anything and anyone are fair game. You are beholden only to the laws of supply and demand.

—

The uneven real-world application of his core philosophy echoes through popular culture today. Although "greed" itself is less baldly embraced than it was a few decades ago, the market principles that my father extended to the realm of love and lust now reach out in every direction. We shop for friends and colleagues on Twitter and Facebook, shop for mates on Tinder, and order everything else we need from Amazon. If the increasing prevalence of open relationships reflects an increasingly liberal society, it also mirrors the ways we've applied the everything-all-the-time excesses of the market system to our love lives. For every tier of service, there is a higher tier of service. For every product, there is an upgrade. For every luxury, there is something even more luxurious out there, somewhere. We no longer need to be encouraged to imagine fancier or better or more. The very existence of a given person, place, or thing now immediately conjures a better, more beautiful, more enticing version of the same. We are so conscribed by the market-driven mind-set that we can no longer experience anything outside of the context of "more" and "better." We can't take things as they are. We have moved on to the upgrade before we've even engaged with what we have right here, right now.

The ultimate fable of this state of being might be Matthew Weiner's *Mad Men,* that dazzling, witty, nostalgic, emotional horror story that captured the imaginations of a certain set of hip urban types when it aired from 2007 until 2015. The show's protagonist, Don Draper, provoked our interest in part because he offered up a sort of American icon of luminous, condescending masculinity. He was a personification of the fables of high capitalism and the discontents of domestic life, embodying the pleasures and perils of the American dream. While actor Jon Hamm had a knack for telegraphing the conflicted, guilt-ridden underbelly of Draper's psyche, his real talent lay in signaling the middle-aged ad man's default state of smooth, swaggery shamelessness. Draper captured the myriad faces of the self-made man over centuries of American history, from the casually destructive impulses of the colonial settlers to the careless conquests of the pioneers to the bold and reckless self-mythologizing initiatives of the Gilded Age.

Yet in spite of his mid-century setting, Draper also presented a very mid-aughts variation on that oft-revived archetype, reflecting the self-consciousness that settled into our bones in the wake of the excesses of the 1980s and '90s. Even as he masterfully manipulated his way upward from class to class, Draper flinched in shame at his great fortune, which was so often procured at others' expense.

His realization of the costs of his pillaging might've shamed even Jay Gatsby. In fact, F. Scott Fitzgerald's narrator, Nick Carraway, might as easily be describing Don Draper when he says of Gatsby, "If personality is an unbroken series of successful gestures, then there was something gorgeous about him, some heightened sensitivity to the promises of life, as if he were related to one of those intricate machines that register earthquakes ten thousand miles away."

This sensitivity is part of what made Don Draper so transfixing: Even in his egocentric plundering of everything in sight, he remained just as vulnerable to the terrors of life as he was to its promises. The deeply unheroic jitteriness at Draper's core was a big piece of what made *Mad Men* such an addictive drama in spite of its relatively low stakes. Because, against a pristine backdrop of sparkling cocktails and jazz and miles of immaculate white carpeting, our handsome leading man lacked all faith in himself and was never truly satisfied. When he wasn't cheating, he was dreaming of cheating. Yet his upgrades seemed to bring him less and less joy. As the beauty and opulence of Draper's surroundings—his office, his possessions, his harem of women—steadily grew, the satisfaction he took in these things eroded proportionately.

Whether he was flirting with you, hiring you, or marrying you, Don Draper was just not that into you. Swooning over Don in spite of yourself—that was the spectator sport of *Mad Men,* like gazing at Italian designer furniture you can't afford. Draper is the $3,000 pink velvet chair that isn't even comfortable to sit on. But we can't take our eyes off him. Even though we know he'll never make us happy, we still like to believe that he might.

Draper had a talent for making a certain flavor of sullen arrogance look appealing—or else his demeanor hinted that happiness itself was overrated, when compared with the allure of brooding. His eyes would go narrow with desire when any woman—his receptionist, his wife, his colleague—put him in his place or, better yet, ignored him completely. He would become openly smug when Megan, his secretary-turned-bride, proved herself an even more efficient and effective version of himself at work. But his face would go flat when she mused about her dreams, or pursued a career path that had nothing to do with him, and therefore didn't adequately flatter his inflated sense of himself.

Don himself was a luxury that flattered us, the viewers. But his value depended on his indifference and the lack of satisfaction he brought to us. "Maybe you aren't good enough for him," we told ourselves, and also, "Maybe you need much more than this. If you can afford something this gorgeous, maybe that means you can afford something even better."

By the show's fifth season, as Don Draper did his best to play house, every other character started acting like the Draper of old: cheating, avoiding suburban responsibility, indulging in workaholism, keeping dark secrets. In their attempts to telegraph restless entitlement, though, most of these characters came off like pouty children. Somehow, only Draper could evoke that terrifying state of having it all but needing more.

Like so many self-invented men before him, he preferred role-playing to real life. He resented other people for their genuine desires and their humanity. As his business partner Roger Sterling put it, when summing up Megan's appeal: "She's a great girl. They're all great girls. At least until they want something."

———

There's another version of this narrative, one that's bleaker, more depraved, and much more popular: the *Fifty Shades of Grey* trilogy, which has now sold more than a hundred million copies worldwide. The book follows the budding relationship between Anastasia Steele, a recent college graduate who's still a virgin (in spite of her drag stage name), and a handsome billionaire named Christian Grey. Early in their interactions, Grey insists that Anastasia agree to a dominant/submissive relationship, requesting that she sign lengthy contracts specifying everything from the forms of punishment she'll endure (leather crops: good; caning: bad) to the amount of exercise she'll do (four hours a week, minimum). Although she's intrigued by Grey's money, his looks, and even his controlling tendencies, Anastasia balks at the contract, is shocked by the S&M equipment in what she refers to as his "red room of pain," and finds it creepy that he insists on never being touched. Christian Grey, in other words, is like Don Draper with helicopters, chilled white wine, and kinky predilections where the chain-smoking, bourbon, and workaholism would normally go.

Late-capitalist fairy tales that double as sexual daydreams aren't new. In one version of the story, a wide-eyed mermaid cleverly disguises her essential self and loses her voice in order to win the heart of a prince (*The Little Mermaid*). In another, a hooker with a heart of gold navigates her way to a happy ending by offering some happy endings of her own (*Pretty*

Woman). Or there's the sassy secretary who shakes her money-maker all the way to the corner office (*Working Girl*).

Fifty Shades of Grey follows this long history of class ascendance via feminine wiles, but does so cleverly disguised as an edgy modern bodice-ripper. Forget that E. L. James's three-book series captures the intricacies of BDSM about as effectively as a "Whip Me" Barbie doll might. Admirers of the series may credit it with liberating female desire by reimagining pornography for ordinary women (and introducing them to the unmatched thrills of leather riding crops and hard spankings). But the story of Anastasia Steele and Christian Grey isn't really about dominance or bondage or even sex or love, despite all the Harlequin Romance–worthy character names.

No, what *Fifty Shades of Grey* offers is a vision of late-capitalist deliverance, the American wet dream. Just as magazines like *Penthouse, Playboy, Chic,* and *Oui* have effectively equated the moment of erotic indulgence with the ultimate consumer release, a totem of the final elevation into amoral privilege, James's trilogy represents the latest installment in the commodified sex genre. The money shot is just that: the moment when our heroine realizes she's been ushered into the hallowed realm of the 1 percent, once and for all.

The fantasy of *Fifty Shades* certainly isn't focused on the erotic sublime. In fact, the sex becomes hopelessly repetitive sometime around the third or fourth of the novels' countless, monotonously naughty encounters. Each dalliance begins with the same come-on: The naïve college graduate Anastasia and the dashing mogul Christian describe their desires to each other with all of the charmless predictability of servers at an Outback Steakhouse. Awkward openers ("I think we've done enough talking for now," "Now let's get you inside and naked") conjure the raw provocation of "How about a Bloomin' Onion to get you started?" Even tougher to take are the coy responses

("Oh my!" "Why, Mrs. Grey, you have a dirty, dirty mouth!" "You're insatiable and so brazen"), repeated with gusto despite the utter lack of shock value in evidence. Reader expectations tick up ever so slightly as Grey issues some bossy commands— Stand here! Undress! Bend over! Spread your legs!—which seem at first blush to foretell a curve in the carnal road. But no such luck. Give or take a blindfold here or a butt plug there, the same hands explore the same places in the same ways with the same results. After the fifteenth or sixteenth time Anastasia and Christian "find [their] release together," they start to resemble amnesiacs doomed to repeat the same boring small talk over and over, as if they are meeting for the first time. By the third volume in the series, as every word out of Christian's mouth ("I see you're very wet, Anastasia") still triggers an overheated response from his paramour ("Holy shit!"), readers may find themselves hissing, "Mix it up a little, for fuck's sake."

Of course the sex is not the main event. The endless manual jimmying and ripped foil packets and escalating rhythms are just foreplay for the real climax, in which Anastasia recognizes that she's destined to abandon her ordinary, middle-class life in favor of the rarefied veal pen of the elite. Until then, like a swooning female contestant on *The Bachelor*, Anastasia is offered breathtaking helicopter and glider rides, heady spins in luxury sports cars, and windswept passages on swift catamarans. She is made to gasp at Christian's plush office, with its sandstone desk and white leather chairs and its stunning vista, or his spacious, immaculate penthouse apartment, with its endless rooms filled with pricey furniture. She is treated to Bollinger pink champagne and grilled sea bass. She is offered a brand-new wardrobe replete with stylish heels and gorgeous gowns and designer bras. She is lavished with diamond jewelry and flowers and a new luxury car of her own.

Soon the numbing parade of luxe brands—Cartier, Cristal, Omega, iPad, iPod, Audi, Gucci—takes on the same dulled impact as endlessly tweaked nipples and repeatedly bound wrists. Curiously (but perhaps not surprisingly), our heroine's responses to these artifacts of her ascendance are as unchangingly enthusiastic as her sexual responses: "Oh, my!" "Yes." "Holy shit!" The superior quality and enormous cost of each item are mulled in excruciating detail.

And just as male-centered pornography seems to feature a particularly clumsy, childish notion of sexiness, the concept of luxury on offer in *Fifty Shades* is remarkably callow. Like an update of the ostentatious, faux-tasteful wealth of *Dynasty*, Christian's penthouse, with its abstract art and dark wood and leather, represents the modern version of enormous flower arrangements and white marble floors and a house staff trussed up in cartoon-butler regalia. No detail of the environment feels organic or specific to Christian himself; instead, it reflects a prescribed aesthetic of wealth that for some reason James approaches with reverence rather than repulsion. Anastasia is on a tour of the world's finest corporate hotels, nothing more or less. By the time this compulsive lifestyle voyeurism starts invading our narrator's routine visits to the bathroom ("The restrooms are the height of modern design—all dark wood, black granite, and pools of light from strategically placed halogens"), the author's veneration of arbitrary signifiers of class has begun to feel grotesque.

Against this backdrop of drooling consumption, Anastasia's total life makeover takes shape. Having just graduated from college, she scales the corporate ladder from assistant to book editor in a matter of weeks, since Christian has thoughtfully purchased the publishing company where she works. When her boss bullies and sexually harasses her, Christian confronts him, has him fired, and installs Anastasia in his place. Her mild protests over this creepy show of power are just for show, of course. The underlying message is that Prince Charming swooped in and saved her from the indignities of the under-class. As if that's not enough, in the third book, *Fifty Shades Freed*, Christian announces that he's going to give the publish-ing company to his new wife, as a wedding present. Career success is thus achieved effortlessly, bequeathed to her by her mate.

There's nothing that money can't buy in this high capital-ist fairy tale, whether it's respect, dignity, or imaginary politi-cal correctness. When Christian leads Anastasia to a palatial Mediterranean-style house with an expansive view of Puget Sound, then explains that he wants to flatten it so he can build a house for the two of them, Anastasia balks. "Why do you want to demolish it?" she asks. "I'd like to make a more sustainable home, using the latest ecological techniques," he replies. His eco-friendliness is just another prescribed life-style choice, of course, a marker of good taste that somehow excuses the obscene excess of tearing a perfectly good house to the ground.

When it comes to wasted resources, though, nothing is quite as luxurious or indulgent as real, live humans who are at your beck and call around the clock. Maybe this is why dozens of pages in the *Fifty Shades* trilogy are dedicated to outlining even the most minor exchanges between this privileged couple and their army of handservants:

"This is a Bolognese sauce. It can be eaten anytime. I'll freeze it." She [the cook Mrs. Jones] smiles warmly and turns the heat right down.

Once we're airborne, Natalia serves us yet more cham-pagne and prepares our wedding feast. And what a feast it is—smoked salmon, followed by roast partridge with a green bean salad and dauphinoise potatoes, all cooked and served by the ever-efficient Natalia.

The waiter has returned with the champagne, which he proceeds to open with an understated flourish.

Sawyer reenters, bearing a paper cup of hot water and a separate tea bag. He knows how I take my tea!

Taylor opens the door and I slide out. He gives me a warm, avuncular smile that makes me feel safe. I smile back.

Like the most loyal and dedicated refugees from *Downton Abbey*, every one of the series' cooks and chauffeurs and security guards and assistants demonstrates polite restraint and obedient discretion in Christian and Anastasia's presence. Each careful movement and gesture, each bland remark and well-timed retreat into the background, evokes the ultimate service-economy fantasy. These interchangeable, faceless humans, whose ubiquity and professionalism we're meant to marvel over repeatedly, are themselves luxury possessions. They are warm but impassive, friendly but reserved, omnipresent but invisible. They register no disputes, no grudges, no rolled eyes, no missed days of work. Nothing seems to bring these shadowy figures more satisfaction than serving Lord Grey and his Lady. Like the growing pile of high-end watches and cars and bracelets that this couple accumulates, their humans start to melt into an idealized mass of blindly loyal subservience, bestowing upon their masters an oversized sense of power.

All of which points to the dark, unspoken moral of the series: *Fifty Shades* offers not just the eroticization of extreme excess, but the commodification of love itself. Christian and Anastasia encounter each other as the most precious of high-end possessions. "You're mine," they tell each other over and over. Like a manicured update to Gollum from *The Lord of the Rings,* Anastasia imagines a world inhabited primarily by covetous rivals. Likewise, Christian panics at Anastasia's smallest exchanges with her boss and male friends, even the coat-check guy at a club. In case we can't grasp that his woman is his most cherished commodity, jealously safeguarded with the mien of a bouncer, he spells it out for us: "You're so precious to me," he tells her in *Fifty Shades Freed.* "Like a priceless asset, like a child."

To Christian, every man alive wants Anastasia. To Anastasia, every woman alive wants Christian. In the logic of the market, each of them must thus be in demand, rare, and highly coveted.

In the real world, such severe possessiveness would create big problems for both parties. But in the fantasy world of *Fifty Shades,* their pathology is recast as its own special kind of indulgence, a way of heightening the sensation of two superior humans looming over the mortal realm like demigods. The slow seduction that culminates in total possession and total power, which the first book sometimes depicts as a dark force to be escaped, is portrayed with accelerating breathlessness and adoration in the second and third volumes. Echoing the lawless privilege of girlie magazines, the so-called control freak within Christian (and, subsequently, Anastasia) demonstrates not just that members of the moneyed class are above the law, but that they exist beyond ordinary ethical guidelines, too. (This, by the way, is also the moral of the higher-brow fore-runner of *Fifty Shades:* Bret Easton Ellis's *American Psycho*—which is a much more self-aware if also somewhat numbing exploration of the nexus between high consumer capitalism and soulless bondage sex, with the significant and oddly more realistic difference that Ellis's alpha-male protagonist is also a serial killer.)

Having complete and total control over every single aspect of your experience, including everyone around you, is the textbook definition of alienation—precisely how human beings are severed from each other and from their own humanity. Perversely, in *Fifty Shades*, this radical isolation is portrayed as a moment of transcendence rather than one of debasement. Armed with an apparently limitless will-to-commodification, our narrator recognizes that anything and everything in the world—objects, people, qualities one would like to appear to have—can be bought for a price. And the qualities of each owned thing reflect more glory back on the owner. "Six stallions, say, I can afford, / Is not their strength my property?" offers Mephistopheles in Goethe's *Faust*. "I tear along, a sporting lord, / As if their legs belonged to me."

But Shakespeare may have captured this spirit of heedless overconsumption best in *Julius Caesar*, when Brutus says of his friend and rival, "The abuse of greatness is when it disjoins remorse from power." Anastasia, who's been showered with priceless goods until she shares her paramour's reckless sense of entitlement, puts it a little differently: "Maybe I need to be restrained."

—

As tedious as *Fifty Shades* becomes, it presents the libidinal titillation and insatiable consumption of *Mad Men* without any of the looming dissatisfaction. Even though both tales offer up a handsome, Gatsby-like embodiment of the American dream, a man who has control issues and a dark past, even though it's at first an open question whether either Christian or Don is capable of real intimacy, vulnerability, or love, *Fifty Shades* answers every haunting question with a shiny, neat, Happily-Ever-After reply. As with Draper, we're at once frustrated and intrigued by Grey's reticence and inability to show up or grow up. Crucially, though, while Draper will most likely cheat, become obsessive about his work, and drink himself into oblivion, Grey remains utterly devoted to Anastasia. He's a mean daddy, a supervillain, a lothario and Gordon Gekko, all rolled into one. Who could ask for anything more?

Draper and Grey present litmus tests of the soul, inversions of the Cinderella story that place the moral burden on the girl in rags clutching the glass slipper. The tension of *Mad Men* lies in the question of whether our heroine (and Draper, in turn) will fall prey to the allure of limitless money, power, and looks, or dig for something deeper and more substantive to sustain her instead. The *Fifty Shades* series, in contrast, begins with a similar question, but it ends in a realm of fantasy where an insatiable desire for more somehow brings an infinite cavalcade of thrills and deep, abiding happiness. "He is mine," Anastasia says over and over again. This is her religion, our religion. We are meant to believe that her possession of this high-end man and this high-end world—and her status as a high-end possession—will be an endless source of deep satisfaction.

Echoes of this belief system are found in the self-mythologizing compulsions around us. Pictured next to his stricken-looking but undeniably gorgeous, expensive import of a wife, with the tacky, gold-plated opulence of Trump Tower in the background, Trump repeatedly reminds us that he represents the ultimate American dream. Everything our imperial patriarch surveys is tremendous. He surrounds himself with people he describes as "high-quality." According to his first-person myth, no matter what he does, he can't help but win, and the only people who disagree with that assessment are losers. But his face tells a different story. Embedded in the orange-spray-tanned folds of his brow, we discover the hidden moral of this tale of luxurious excess and limitless power: There is no satisfaction in reckless, excessive accumulation. The more you have, the more you want. There is never enough.

"Rather than a tale of greed, the history of luxury could more accurately be read as a record of emotional trauma," writes Alain de Botton in his book *Status Anxiety*, efficiently summing up Draper, Grey, and Trump in one blow. "It is the legacy of those who have felt pressured by the disdain of others to add an extraordinary amount to their bare selves in order to signal that they too may lay a claim to love." Anything secured through such means—whether it's love or lust or safety or a $3,000 Italian watch or a gorgeous wife who grimaces every time you look away—promises limited returns of joy. Thus our insatiable protagonists are forced to forge on in search of a new fix. The beauty and the ultimate value of a story like *Mad Men* lies in its repeated insistence that unless we stop searching for more, we'll never truly find happiness or peace. Likewise, the danger of *Fifty Shades*—and the danger of the self-serving myth at the center of the Trump brand—lies in its inability to recognize the pathology at the heart of the fantasy it presents.

As the philosopher Alan Watts puts it in *The Book*, "When the outcome of a game is certain, we call it quits and begin another." Don Draper sums up this process when he tells some Dow executives: "You're happy because you're successful, for now. But what is happiness? It's a moment before you need more happiness." This sentiment echoes the darkness at the center of *The Great Gatsby*, in which Fitzgerald makes it clear that most ambition is driven by a mirage, a focus on "the orgiastic future that year by year recedes before us."

When the most prominent love stories of our times also serve as cautionary tales about wealth and ego-driven restlessness, you have to wonder if there's not some essential sickness encoded in our cultural DNA. As your stature grows to that of an oligarch or a demigod, you require bigger prizes and distractions. This is why Gatsby sets his sights on Daisy Buchanan: a goal worthwhile precisely for its impossibility. Eventually, though, Gatsby is subsumed by his own talent for self-invention. Like Draper, he becomes a cipher, a shadow of someone else's idea of happiness.

This is the shared fantasy in our bloodstream: An ideal life is one spent in a state of constant titillation, a never-ending foreplay session, an eternal flirtation with "more," a superhero cliffhanger, the luxury goods that make you crave even more luxury. Our ghosts—and our villains, which are the same as our heroes, which are the same as our leaders—are those who have a knack for perpetuating this titillation. They loom forever in a state of near-erotic agitation without ever arriving at their destination.

But there's a freedom in never being present enough to feel disappointment, never being connected enough to fear loss, never feeling alive enough to worry about growing old and dying. To remain titillated over the course of *Mad Men* or *Fifty Shades* or *The Great Gatsby* or indeed the Trump presidency, happiness and true love must never enter the picture. Instead, contempt and self-doubt and fear are kicked up repeatedly, inciting the frenzied, volatile state that we, in our immaturity, equate with youth and desire and excitement. Fear means we are on our way somewhere important. Anxiety means that greatness will be here soon. Greed is good because it keeps you restless and hungry.

In an age of narcissism, it's only fitting that our heroes be deeply jittery, with an unconscious wish to remain that way. Their elaborate game of make-believe can be found at the heart of every conquistador's tale. By focusing on a receding, elusive goal, we have the luxury of remaining haunted forever.

playing house

A few days before I moved into my older boyfriend's house, we were talking on the phone and then suddenly we were arguing and before I knew it, I had smashed the handset of my phone to pieces against the floor of my apartment. This man could infuriate me in a matter of seconds, but he also held the promise of exactly the kind of life I wanted. He was mature and settled. He was charismatic, grown-up, full of ideas. But nothing he said made any sense to me. He knew how to sound like an adult, worldly and omniscient, but quickly enough I found holes in his speeches. Most of the time, I pretended not to notice them.

He was renting a nice little bungalow with a great view. All of his furniture was carefully chosen from the Pasadena flea market. His stereo had excellent speakers, and the sound was

always perfectly balanced with just the right mix of treble and
bass. The walls held creepy Virgin Marys and old paintings,
the kinds of things that seasoned, thoughtful adults like himself had on their walls. He would buy cool old ashtrays at the
flea market, for guests, he said, for guests with cigarettes and
guests with blunts. But something about his home was never
quite right. Everything was minimal and perfectly placed, but
covered in a film of dust. He had been an actor and a dancer,
and now he was studying to become a lawyer. But at heart, he
was an artist (this is what I told myself) and a thinker. His life
was constructed in anticipation of an audience.

I fell in lockstep with this anticipatory energy, replacing his
dying plants with living ones, buying more and more plants
and rearranging them on the front porch, where they got too
much sun and had to be watered constantly, and then buying
more plants for the backyard. I washed off the tables, washed
the glass on the creepy old paintings, washed the wood floors
on my hands and knees, scrubbed the bathrooms. But somehow the house never felt clean. There wasn't enough sunshine.
I took photos of the big front window, proving to myself that
it was a sunny place, but even in the photographs the sunshine
looked weak, ambivalent.

Each week his ex-wife would come to the house to pick up
her dog, Bingo, which he called *their* dog, as if a dog could
be split equally between two people living in different places.
He would hide in the back of the house when she knocked
and then let herself in the front door with her key. The whole
arrangement was absurd. She had a key to our house? She
could just let herself in? But I'd answered the door a few times,
and that was even worse. I would shower just to answer the
door. I would put on makeup. I would second-guess my tone:
Too friendly? Too fake? And she seemed nervous. It felt like
a show I had to rehearse for. I didn't like having an audience

of one. I couldn't prove everything I wanted to prove: That she was bad and I was good. That she was old and I was new. That she had made a big mistake and her leftovers were being treasured by someone healthy enough to recognize the value of what she had left behind.

I wasn't up to the role. I didn't understand my character's motivation. I had lost the thread. An hour before she was supposed to arrive, I would rearrange the plants on the front porch, pruning away the brown parts, rewatering everything. The plants put on a better show than I did. They said, "This house is happy now," in a more convincing tone than my own voice could manage. But once she left, with her neat blonde hair and her cute sweatpants and her thin frame, once she departed with Bingo (who clearly loved his mother more than he loved us) and drove home to the down-to-earth, regular, lovable younger guy she'd discovered as her marriage was falling apart, the house felt less happy. Once she left, I could see that my boyfriend was just her condescending ex-husband, and our cozy bungalow was just their old house. I could see the places where her furniture was missing. I was living in those empty spaces, sprucing up darkness that would never lift. I was haunting their failures, a bystander, asking my boyfriend for more details of their bad wedding and their bad life together, as if reworking an unworkable proof.

Soon after she left, her condescending ex-husband would go to the kitchen to make us margaritas. He made them with pure tequila and lime juice and triple sec, but the balance was never right. His drinks tasted like limes and rubbing alcohol, filled to the brim of martini glasses, always spilling over the sides. We would sit on the porch, in chairs selected for audience impact rather than comfort. We would sip our too-strong drinks and I would try to start a lively discussion, just weighty enough, just intense enough to get us going. But this man sitting next to me was just someone else's condescending ex-husband, so he rarely took the bait. He got up to fix the balance on the stereo; it was too loud, now it was too soft. He got up to move his chair; the sun was shining in his eyes. He got up to get his lumbar pillow; his back was hurting again. He got up to get another drink; he'd already finished his first one. He got up to go to the bathroom. He got up to check his messages. He got up to grab a book he wanted to tell me about, something that was beneath him and beneath me, something new age, something with God in the title, something self-helpy. I started to notice that everything he said came out of a book he'd read. I started to see that he couldn't improvise. He needed his script. He was angry all the time. He was furious at his ex. He couldn't believe she'd left him for that schlubby guy. I was a bystander in this drama. The script demeaned both of us.

I didn't allow myself to acknowledge this. Instead I focused on fixing things, cleaning things up. I would be more patient. I would buy more plants. I would hide the next time, instead of answering the door. I would heal all wounds with my superior love for this man, who was slowly revealing himself to be very difficult to love, a plant getting way too much sunlight, a plant that would rather just wither up and die.

"Remind me to do this more often," he'd say, after lighting a joint. Then he'd laugh a tight laugh. He'd throw his head back—everything he did was theatrical—but it was still tight, still angry. He was obsessed with relaxing, but he never seemed relaxed. I didn't let myself notice this. I didn't let myself take in how dissatisfied he always was, how distracted, how he could never just look me in the eyes—that thing he did the night we met, which I remembered so well, that thing I got fixated on, how he met my gaze and didn't look away. He had lost the ability to look me in the eyes. He could only do it when he was mad. He was mad a lot. I looked away. I washed the floors again.

There was a propulsive energy to that time. I worked hard to make things better. It took a lot of work; everything took work. I was unemployed, so I had time and energy to pour into this terrible doomed project. But all of the thoughts I kept myself from thinking would settle in at night. I would climb into my side of the bed and turn my back to him and I would think, "I have to leave. I have to get out of here. This is torture. I have to dump him." He would get up to tuck the blankets in more tightly at the bottom of the bed, so it felt like I was being pinned down by a net. I would kick the blanket up at the bottom until I was free.

In the morning, I told myself, "This is how you feel when you're making a real commitment. This is how it is when you're in love and you're not going anywhere. Love takes hard work." I could fix this. I could make his ex regret leaving, and make him glad she left. I could make Bingo the dog love me more. I could make the plants thrive, even the ones turning brown, even the ones covered in aphids, scary horror-show bugs I'd never seen before. I had so many challenges ahead of me. That felt good. I would work even harder.

—

One day, my boyfriend called his ex and asked her to bring back a shelf she'd taken away. It was his shelf and he needed it, he said. When she brought the shelf back, he and I were sitting at the kitchen table. He decided he wouldn't hide this time, since we were mostly out of sight. She brought the shelf into the living room and left the front door open, so we could see her through the kitchen window. She took out some wood cleaner and cleaned the shelf right there, so that she didn't leave it dusty for us.

Watching her clean the shelf, I saw: She took care of him in ways I would never manage. There we were, each of us preparing for an audience, but really she was the star, even now, even long gone. This was a woman who could work with what she had. She brought the magic to that house. When she left, the magic left with her.

He laughed at her for cleaning the shelf. He tried to say that it was annoying, he could see that now, how annoying she was about everything, such a control freak. I tried to join in but my heart wasn't in it. When she got into her car and drove away, the sunshine dimmed a little. I wanted to follow her to her new house in the Valley, to sit with her new boyfriend and bear witness to their life, which was real. They weren't just playing house like we were, waiting for more. They had everything they needed. How did that feel?

I might've imagined I would land somewhere like that eventually. Or maybe I suspected that I would never be worthy of that kind of a life. Either way, I probably should have cultivated more empathy for that man, who was so clearly in a lot of pain. But I still remember how good it felt to smash the handset of my phone into pieces. I hadn't even moved in yet and I was already furious. I was in love and I already hated the guy. I knew I shouldn't move in with him. But it almost felt satisfying to hate him. My disappointment had a clear source. I would try to make things perfect and I would fail, over and over again. I couldn't just love someone and be loved back. That was too easy. That didn't feel right. I was more familiar with dissatisfaction. I was more at home with longing. As I moved my things into that dusty, tiny, haunted house, I looked around and thought, "This will never be enough." It was exactly what I wanted.

delusion at the gastropub

I f anything marks our arrival on the dystopian shores of gross overconsumption, it's the foodie movement. Because it takes a lot of late-capitalist pixie dust to turn the basics of subsistence into coveted luxuries. The brazen marketing of designer water at $5 per bottle, flown in from Fiji or the Alps—or better yet, filled from a local municipal tap—may have been the first red flag, signaling the modern public's staggering ability to suspend its disbelief or simply to miss the basic thrust of manufactured demand.

But if one trait characterizes upper-middle-class citizens with lots of disposable income, it's their tireless compulsion to dispose of that income in fresh new ways. The more pedestrian the product in question, the greater its seeming potential to evoke untold volumes of feeling and meaning. A few centuries into the future, inhabitants of a ravaged globe may look back on this time as the crucial moment at which delusional fervor around unremarkable, overpriced things reached its apex. The glorification of food seems understandable enough, at first glance. Everybody's got to eat. And as with any other animal urge or act of survival—masticate, copulate, procreate, repeat—it's not exactly an achievement to move this activity to the center of one's value system. What upper-middle-class college student doesn't emerge from six months abroad in Barcelona swearing fealty to the crown of *jamón ibérico*? What leisurely plutocrat isn't tempted to throw his energies into a hobby with immediate built-in payoffs, like becoming an overnight expert on the expensive aged cheeses of the world? What better pastime for a wealthy faux-hippie housewife than raising egg-laying hens (they're adorable!) or learning to pickle the organic vegetables her child is growing at his pricey progressive preschool? Like so many other consumer hobbies, such extracurricular foodie activities are easy to engage in, relatively cheap, and come with their own built-in gustatory and social rewards.

Those who require that their hobbies also have a heroic sheen can turn to the lovingly itemized ideological bases of the so-called food revolution. A long train of exposés and manifestos detail the myriad ways our foodstuffs have been too long tainted by chemical manipulations, resource-intensive factory farming, overprocessing, and general tastelessness. The solution, from the consumer's standpoint, is to repair all this systemic damage with better informed, more locally minded shopping. To combat the epidemic of fast food (and the kindred American plague of obesity), we've been schooled in the virtues of "slow food," aka "locavore" cuisine, aka organic and regional produce, meats, and dairy products. All of which is worthy enough, as far as our individual consumption goes.

We're all likelier to lead healthy, slim, fulfilling, and flavorful lives when we nourish ourselves on farmers' market fare, aren't we? Not to mention that we feel better about ourselves as agents of ethical change.

Yet there's not much evidence that this trend for artisanal cuisine has produced anything close to a more just, affordable, and robust food economy. If anything, it has driven our already class-segmented food system into still greater polarities, with privileged access to rabbit larb and Japanese uni at one end of the spectrum, and a wasteland of overprocessed, cheap, and empty grub at the other.

Nonetheless, foodies have learned to transform the self-indulgent habit of spending more than $200 on a single meal into an intellectual and cultural badge of honor—a chance to loudly advertise their great taste in public, as they remark on the bright or redolent or flavorful undertones of whatever anxiously plated concoction they've just savored. Those with money to burn will always find creative ways to paint even their most decadent indulgences as enlightened, discriminating, and honorable. And those who provide such indulgences are probably wise to collude in this fantasy.

Of course, the fantasy itself grows more baroque and involuted as the foodie cult nets an ever-greater number of well-heeled recruits. In spite of the self-congratulatory earthiness that foodie culture tends to favor ("I just really love food," earnest foodies will confess, seemingly unaware that most of humankind shares their passion), its overwrought quasi-religiosity picks up right where the rise of designer bottled water left off. "Food is everything!" foodies declare, or "Live to eat, not eat to live!"—battle cries apparently aimed at shaking the rest of the populace out of its imagined hunger strike. But purchasing a meal at Chez Panisse or Momofuku or Trois Mec is not enough. One must dine at all of Eater's "essential"

restaurants, murmur reverently of Michelin stars, and speak in
an authoritative, *Top Chef*–tutored tongue on the importance
of balancing sourness and sweetness and umami in every single bite. The solemnly important task of delivering "thoughtful" and "inventive" food to every semi-hip town in America
has been accomplished, and food culture mavens have offi-
cially overshot their mark: Eating out now means being served
sweetmeats on a slab of brick while listening to the neighbor-
ing table grouse about the inadequate "acidity" of their last
plate in the self-serious tones of film critics rolling their eyes at
Terrence Malick's latest clumsy offerings.

And don't forget the importance of chronicling the eating
experience. If eating is a deeply private and emotional activity,
laced with personal meaning and nostalgia, then the Yelp restaurant review corpus is our communal diary, in which each
diarist struggles mightily to mimic the hauteur of the establish-
ment food critic. Take this review of a hot Italian restaurant in
a fashionable neighborhood of Los Angeles:

> We ordered the chicken liver crostone, the octopus, and
> the chopped salad "amigliorata" to start. The chicken
> liver was ludicrous—airy and creamy in texture, and
> absolutely rich with flavor. It came with thick crusty
> hunks of grilled bread and a tart black plum mostarda,
> a thoughtful accompaniment to the decadent liver. The
> octopus was tender and toothsome, served over a bed
> of black barley, roasted carrots, and red onion—a nice,
> earthy dish with some balancing brightness.

Or how about this one, for a ramen joint nearby:

> Everything in the Ozu pork ramen was on point, except
> for the broth. The pork was tender and flavorful, the ajit-

suke egg was cooked to perfection, and I liked the tangy flavor added by the mizuna on top. The broth was on the lighter side—not to my liking (I like the fattier broths of Santouka Ramen)—but what made it fail for me was the lack of depth. Even lighter broths need that umami flavor to be good, and Ozu's broth fell flat on its face on this dimension. . . . I will not come back to Ozu East Kitchen until they add a richer, fattier pork broth.

Both reviews brandish the standard terms of food critics and blogs—ludicrous, decadent, earthy, brightness, umami—all mixed and matched in an invocation of devotion resembling an old Latin Mass.

And that's not to mention the self-righteousness, which elevates a mundane consumer choice to the level of a heroic stand against . . . a ramen joint whose broth was insufficiently fatty? The Yelp reviewing customer emerges not as an audience member, bystander, or faceless nobody holding a wallet, but as someone central to the entire production, the star of the show, even. This incoherence of self goes straight to the heart of what makes foodie culture such a vibrant manifestation of consumerist bewilderment. Lured into a world of luxe commodities by their taste buds, their nostalgia, and a growing sense of their own insignificance, high-end consumers do much more than simply misjudge a basic exchange of lucre for product. They come to identify intimately with the embrace or rejection of said product (*I like the fattier broths of Santouka Ramen*). They do so as if the world turns on their appraisals, awaits their Yelp verdicts like an anxious crowd in Rome waiting for the cardinals to elect a new Pope.

The foodie identity can be so completely constructed by its various deeply felt products (the broths of Santouka! the roasted chickens of Waxman's!) that it transforms itself from

a statement of allegiance—like the sports teams you follow or
the bands you like—and enters into the realm of the political. Being a foodie means taking a vow to save the Earth,
to save small organic farms, and to save poor, overweight,
undernourished people from themselves. But then, empty self-
righteousness has always paired nicely with a rich sense of
entitlement. That earthy taste of stone soup, drizzled in an
unctuous snake oil.

For an elevated sampling of these flavor profiles, look no
further than the pages of *A Taste of Generation Yum* by Eve
Turow (2015). Turow explains, from a conveniently ahistori-
cal perch, that the food revolution began when millennials
surveyed their parents' very bad food choices and demanded
something better. Yes, millennial foodies, whom Turow and
others refer to as "Yummers," are single-handedly driving the
foodie movement with their hard-earned dollars. Or not so
hard-earned, since, as Turow herself alleges, 38 percent of
young adults were unemployed in 2013. These valiant Yummers are spending their boomer parents' dough.

And even though so many of the millennials Turow describes
don't have jobs and are living off their parents' money, they're
special because their "tastes are limitless." They're not *just*
spending most of their money on fussily plated calf tongue;
they're eschewing straight jobs so they can pursue their dreams
of "harvesting clams or milking goats or tilling the land."

All of which can only suggest that millennials care more
deeply about food than anyone else ever has. "Young people
are actively, purposefully integrating food into their lives and
giving it daily attention—and value—in a different proportion
than any previous generation," Turow writes. Members of certain agrarian societies—not to mention a boomer army of Julia
Child and *Joy of Cooking* fanatics—would surely beg to dif-

fer. But then, millennials aren't the first generation to declare themselves the driving force behind a movement that started fifty years before they were born, and they won't be the last.

Yet as David Kamp suggests in *The United States of Arugula: The Sun-Dried, Cold-Pressed, Extra Virgin Story of the American Food Revolution* (2006), the developments that characterize today's foodscape began with the rise of fine dining and French cuisine in the States after World War II, helped along by James Beard, Julia Child, and Craig Claiborne, who popularized fresh-baked bread and the art of fine home cooking at a time when women's magazines encouraged housewives to embed canned mandarin oranges in lime Jell-O. What some view as a sudden food revolution is in fact the product of a long, slow evolution of tastes that's taken place over the course of seventy-odd years, with new restaurant and food trends arising like clockwork every few years to replace the previous batch. Or as Nora Ephron succinctly put it in her 2006 *New Yorker* essay, "Serial Monogamy," "This was right around the time that arugula was discovered, which was followed by endive, which was followed by radicchio, which was followed by frisée, which was followed by the three M's—mesclun, mâche, and microgreens—and that, in a nutshell, is the history of the past forty years from the point of view of lettuce."

Reducing what might otherwise be viewed as a "revolution" to a shift in trends of taste is not to understate the enormous quantity of cash in play today, though. No wonder the preferred view—advanced by those with a stake in food's "revolutionary" status—is far more portentous than either Kamp's or Ephron's. But then, if your dinner isn't revolutionary, how can you possibly justify spending a week's salary on it?

—

Here's where any argument about the fatuousness of the foodie necessarily teeters: When you actually *taste* that coffee, or those prosciutto-wrapped figs. A few minutes in a pricey cheese shop, speaking to a smart person who spends all her time thinking and talking about cheese, has a way of convincing you that high-quality fromage is one of the primary pleasures of life, worthy of its price, particularly if those dollars go into the hands of smart enthusiasts and the gorgeous, enlightened, loving dairy farmers of your vivid imaginations. (This seduction is a big piece of foodie culture's appeal: We aren't just shoving tasty stuff into our faces, we're embracing and supporting some down-to-earth farmer who might count as a kind of a neighbor.) It's all so sexy and sensual and honorable-seeming: We care about our bodies and we care about the Earth and its products, we tell ourselves. Not like those corn-syrup-swilling slobs sitting next to us on the train, gorging themselves on the products of unsustainable industrial monoculture.

This is the ugly class subtext of our earnest adoration of that Humboldt Fog chevre wheel with a layer of "edible vegetable ash." Our hard-won locavore connoisseurship satisfies our senses and bestows upon us, via its $25-a-pound price tag, the feeling that we've paid tithes to the church of gourmet eating. But more than that, it separates us from the less sainted, the less antioxidized, and, meaningfully, the less wealthy among us.

This separation is savored privately, like a slice of eighteen-month-aged Manchego unloosed from a stainless steel double-wide fridge at midnight. But it's also distinctly social. As William Deresiewicz wrote in *The New York Times* in 2012, foodie culture

> is a badge of membership in the higher classes, an ideal example of what Thorstein Veblen, the great social critic

of the Gilded Age, called conspicuous consumption. It is a vehicle of status aspiration and competition, an ever-present occasion for snobbery, one-upmanship and social aggression. (My farmers' market has bigger, better, fresher tomatoes than yours.) Nobody cares if you know about Mozart or Leonardo anymore, but you had better be able to discuss the difference between ganache and couverture.

The so-called food revolution may include many Earth-friendly initiatives—the emphasis on organic, pesticide-free products; the local farm-to-table efforts; the transition to vegetarian, vegan, or just mostly plant-based diets; the crop rotation and sustainable, environmentally friendly practices of small farms; the efforts to reduce food waste, etc. But the broad impact of elevating food to a rarefied luxury good has wide-reaching negative consequences for the planet. Because for every local organic farm churning out hormone-free basil butters and heirloom beets, there are countless other elite consumers feasting on foods flown in from around the globe. As Dan Barber points out in *The Third Plate: Field Notes on the Future of Food* (2014), the second that those locally sourced lamb chops run out at the foodie farm-to-table restaurant of the aspirational classes' fever dreams, the obliging restaurateur must secure a backup source that's perhaps less local and less blessed by the purist foodie gods.

For the food revolution to save the Earth (or at least not hasten its demise), Barber argues, our whole way of thinking about food needs to shift. Instead of chasing fickle consumer tastes and allowing the gods of supply and demand to rape the Earth and dredge the seas until all of our ecosystems are utterly destroyed, we have to learn to appreciate foods that can be grown or raised sustainably, foods that support and enrich the environment. The next food preferences (those that might eventually graduate to trends) need to be carefully selected by chefs who forgo the sorts of "luxury" foods that are leaving their habitats denuded and unbalanced for more pragmatic choices—eco-friendly farmed fish, say, or plants that filter toxins from the soil or replete the soil's much-needed nitrogen. As easy as it is to be cynical about politically correct, pretentious menus that read more like essays, the choices we make now as consumers will affect how we're able to eat—not to mention survive—in the future.

Because if foodie culture wants to take credit for the rise of organic, sustainable, cruelty-free farming, it's also going to have to take the blame for making us crave tasty slices of grass-fed venison and baby corn (a plate of food requiring an obscene and wanton waste of natural resources), or sushi rolls packed with four varieties of endangered fish, flown in from three different oceans. Devoted foodies may choose to believe that shoving pickled shishito peppers and chicken livers and herbed goat cheese into their gullets represents a divine embrace of earthbound pleasures. But like most other bourgeois hobbies, this one carries considerable costs. Not only has the elevation of food to luxury created absurd expectations around a dimension of survival that might otherwise involve as few exotic elements as possible, but it's also warped our understanding of how we exist on the Earth and how we coexist with our fellow earthlings, the cuddliest and cutest of which also tend to taste really good the younger and lazier and the more stuffed with organic hazelnuts they are.

Take a deep dive into those giant, ever-prevalent Blue Apron boxes, filled with tiny plastic bags of purple basil and frozen slabs of minced lamb, and you'll see that even mere commoners now feast like kings and queens. It's time to acknowledge that our enthusiasms have taken us too far. We can't continue eating most of the animals we've overbred and forced into short, filthy, miserable lives.

Once the world's population sneaks up toward eleven billion, many have argued that we will require the supersized yields of industrial farming—which means that even though we might prefer small-batch brie from a darling mom-and-pop dairy farm in Vermont, we still have to vehemently support curbing the environmental recklessness of our industrial farms while we're at it. As nice as it is to have organic free-range everything on your plate, imbuing that choice with deeper meaning and a larger sense of righteousness without addressing the bigger picture of how humanity feeds itself is like boarding a private jet and then congratulating yourself for not giving the highly polluting commercial airline industry any of your hard-earned dollars.

But beyond the fantastical idealism of foodie culture, there's the simple fact that cooking a decent meal or dining at the right restaurant is an act of leisure-class consumption rather than a heroic or courageous feat to build your entire identity around. As former food critic John Lanchester asserts in *The New Yorker,* our choices about food are nowhere near the most important political choices we make. "If these tiny acts of consumer choice are the most meaningful actions in our lives," Lanchester writes, "perhaps we aren't thinking and acting on a sufficiently big scale." He takes it a step further. "Imagine that you die and go to Heaven and stand in front of a jury made up of Thomas Jefferson, Eleanor Roosevelt, and Martin Luther King, Jr. Your task would be to compose yourself, look them in the eye, and say, 'I was all about fresh, local, and seasonal.'"

Food is personal. It's sensual, it's nostalgic, it's political. But contrary to the slogans of our officious foodie overlords, food is not everything. Wearing our foodie status as a badge of

honor makes sense only if we're prioritizing food advocacy—
from promoting sustainable farming practices to reducing
food waste to embracing and popularizing more sustainable
crops to making healthy food more affordable to the poor—
over our indulgence in wildly expensive plates of exotic fare.
Before we dive into another dish of bluefin or veal brains or
carrots with a 15.2 Brix reading, we should consider how we'll
look fifty years from now to the inhabitants of an overfished,
polluted planet: decadent, callous, delusional, and above all,
deeply unsavory.

adults only

dults are not always so fun. Sometimes I go to parties filled with mature people who know things and act their age and I'm quickly filled with despair. I walk in the door and greet the host and mill about, but in the pit of my stomach I know that leaving home was a huge mistake. I will not be surprised and delighted. I will not learn something new. I will not even enjoy the sound of my own voice. I will be lulled into a state of excruciating paralysis and self-hatred and other-people hatred.

Let's be honest, some days, sensible middle-aged urban liberal adult professionals are the most tedious people in the world. I know that I should feel grateful that these people, my peers, are enlightened, that they listen to NPR and read *The Atlantic,* that they join book clubs and send their kids to the progressive preschool and the Italian immersion magnet. I should feel cheered by the fact that I know human beings who hold national grants to improve government policy on something or other, or who work with troubled teenagers. These people are informed and intelligent. These are the people I should *want* to know.

But I am an ingrate. My lack of gratitude might be a product of despair, which pairs badly with my lukewarm Hawaiian-surfer-themed microbrew. I should feel thankful that almost everyone at this party skimmed *The New York Times* this morning. I should feel glad that they read the latest book by Donna Tartt so they can tell me that they didn't think it was all that good, in the vaguest terms possible. I should see this as an opportunity to hear myself say words out loud about the latest book by Donna Tartt, throwing in specific arguments about what qualifies as good writing and what makes a book worthwhile—but without insulting anyone or swearing for no reason or making spit fly out of my mouth in the process. But I might get long-winded and say too much. There is a palpable pressure to never say too much here. There is an imaginary egg timer for every comment. The sand runs out, the eyes go dead.

I should be glad just to be here, to be invited out of the house so I can stand beside a table of food I didn't personally prepare, all of those bad salads with the quinoa and the mushy bits of avocado and the overcooked pasta and the giant lumps of bland feta and the little bits of green stuff that has no discernible flavor. I should feel thankful to be slowing down in sync with this diverse and informed tribe, to be aging gracefully among these mild-mannered international humans in their denim shirts, in their linens, in their comfortable shoes, in their terrible newsboy caps, holding their beers until they sweat and grow warm, sipping their glasses of Pinot Grigio but never having a second glass, helping themselves to an intolerably weak margarita that needs a sign that says ADULTS ONLY on the side because it is served in small blue Dixie cups and it looks and tastes exactly like lemonade. After one cup I quickly calculate that I will need to drink the whole pitcher of Adults Only Lemonade to catch a buzz. For a while I try to do this.

But catching a buzz is not the point at a gathering like this one. In fact, the point is to *avoid* catching a buzz. Sure, these professional adults once used to drink too much and say the wrong things, when they were much younger. But they've accumulated enough experience over the years to realize that the more appropriate thing is to resist such an impulse, to file down their more unsightly edges, to blend in. It's not that they don't still have unpopular opinions and bad urges. They're just mature enough to know these things make people uncomfortable, end friendships, hijack careers. You can't go to a party and act like you're at a party. You're too old for that. You might speak out of turn or contradict yourself or offend someone. That's not how adults do it.

Among adults, everything must exist within clearly defined boundaries and limits: No heels are uncomfortably high (and everyone leaves their shoes at the front door anyway), no music is too loud, no lipstick is too dark, no food is too spicy, no drink is too strong, no conversation lasts too long. No one yells or points or mocks, even just for fun. No one has any obvious personality disorders. No one is quiet or seems lonely. No one looks desperate or sweaty. No one is inappropriate or has lipstick on her teeth or is wearing overly large statement jewelry. No one is calling attention to himself for no reason. No one is anxious to cause a stir. No one feels trapped, not outwardly. Such feelings—the longing, the anger, the envy— all of that should have been lifted away decades ago, evaporated, whisked away by linen blends and decaf coffee drinks and probiotics. Everyone should appear calm and properly hydrated now. Everyone should claim to feel just right in their terrible shorts, their legs crossed like Europeans, their temples graying by the minute, their pleasant expressions saying, "I see your point, I understand, that is *also* true." Everyone should be smiling with their eyes and talking with their hands.

They'd like more pasta, but they could also live without it.

I can't do it. The quiet restraint, the lack of discernible needs or desires, the undifferentiated sea of dry-cleaned nothingness, the small sips, the half-smiles, the polite pauses, the autopilot nodding. It feels like we're all voluntarily erasing ourselves, as if that's the only appropriate thing to do.

So I sit in the backyard, on the grass, alone, away from the adults. I think about what it means to blend into the scenery until you disappear. I wonder why that's the point.

A dog approaches with an oblong toy made of clear, melon-colored plastic. The dog gets up in my face. The dog has strong needs, strong preferences. The dog is an individual, demanding and unique. The dog's breath smells like dead fish.

I grab the slobbery stick it's clutching, but the dog's teeth are locked onto it. I hold tight to one end of the slippery thing, which looks like a translucent penis in a ribbed condom. The dog won't let go. The dog is conflicted. The dog wants me to throw the toy, but it also wants to retain possession of the toy, forever and ever. It wants excitement, but it also wants to savor the thrill of ownership. The dog doesn't mind contradicting itself. The dog is impolite. The dog's eyes are bloodshot. The dog wants everything, all at once.

The dog drops the toy, and I'm holding the slimy thing in my hands, and then the dog lunges for it again and almost bites my hand, because my having the toy seemed *not okay* for a second there. "DROP it," I say, in a less-than-polite tone. "DROP IT DROP IT." The dog looks me in the eye and chomps and doesn't let go. "DROP. IT." I growl in a low voice. The dog drops it.

I toss a wet dick across the grass for hours. The grass is artificial. The dog is never quite satisfied. I feel good. This is much better.

stuffed

t's just stuff." This is what my father told a reporter as he watched his condo burn down a year before his death. A faulty attic fan had sparked a fire during the day while he was at work. By the time he got home, half of his worldly possessions had been reduced to ash. The reporter referred to him as "stoical," but his reaction made sense to me. How do you measure what your stuff means to you, in a moment like that?

After my dad's death, the fire looked more like an omen. I was supposed to sort through the boxes of his remaining things stored at my mom's house, but I couldn't bring myself to do it. I would spend a few minutes sifting through photographs of girlfriends I'd never even met or shuffling through books about World War II mixed in with new age tomes about the flowering of self-love, but soon it felt invasive, like trying to unpack my dad's conflicted soul from a tower of boxes. I felt sure that he wouldn't have wanted to leave so many personal traces of himself behind.

Two years after his death, a tree fell on my mother's house and broke through the ceiling in the corner of a bedroom where the boxes of his things were stacked. A few years after that, half of his stuff was stolen from an upstairs closet when my mom's house was robbed. It was as though my dad, from some remote perch, was helping us do what we couldn't—get rid of his possessions once and for all.

No such luck. Today there are still a few boxes of his stuff in my mom's house. No one feels like deciding what to throw out and what to keep. It's just stuff, as my dad said, some of it decades old. But somehow the stakes feel higher now than ever.

—

We first-world humans have always had a conflicted relationship with our belongings. Decades ago, most people owned a lot less stuff. But with the rise of the mall in the 1970s and '80s, shopping became a legitimate leisure activity for the middle class, and people started to accumulate a lot of unnecessary junk. By the 1990s, lower manufacturing costs meant that the struggle to avoid getting crushed under your mountains of cheap things was real. Creative storage solutions were all the rage; enter the Container Store (founded in 1978) and Hold Everything (founded in 1983), followed by the rise of the professional organizer. The early 2000s ushered in the decluttering movement: Your stuff wasn't supposed to be stored in plain sight anymore. Closets became status pieces, the way kitchens are now. The rich hired closet designers, bought houses based on how many closets they had. The non-rich stuffed their gigantic CD towers into their closets with the rest of their unsightly possessions. By the late 2000s, reality shows about hoarders made clinging to our stuff look less like a quirk and more like a sickness. The arrival of cloud storage in the 2010s completed our journey to minimalism. Suddenly books and CDs and photo albums, our former tokens of self-expression, looked more like archaic clutter. From Pinterest to Instagram to the pages of *Real Simple* and *Dwell*, the message rang clear: Your best life could only be lived against a backdrop as pristine and uncluttered as an art gallery.

Thus was the shiny, empty stage set for a new tidying messiah. Marie Kondo's *The Life-Changing Magic of Tidying Up*, published in October 2014, spoke to the heart of the modern human. Who doesn't love the prim, already-quite-clean sound of "tidying up"? Who doesn't crave life-changing magic in all its forms? But Kondo's real message was far more revolutionary than that. "Life truly begins only after you have put your house in order," she decreed in the preface of her 2016 follow-up book, *Spark Joy*. This was the dramatic language that helped her first book sell millions of copies worldwide. But you had to wonder: Wouldn't adding another book to your shelf, alongside the first one, amount to accumulating more unnecessary junk?

Because the heart and soul of Kondo-izing was never her road map to categorizing and storing. Kondo's central, underlying message—her haunting subtext and the primary reason for her massive popularity—was that most of the stuff we own is not only pointless, unnecessary, and burdensome, but holds us back from growing into fully realized human beings. Our extra stuff is not a sign of our prosperity, it's a sign of our impoverishment.

Of course Kondo never would've become a global superstar if she used such negative language. Instead, she embraces poetic, almost ecstatic terms for letting go of excess: At one point the collector's edition of her book was titled *Experience the Pulsing Magic of Cleaning Up Every Day.* And the experience of reading Kondo's books *does* induce a kind of pulsing magic. Her optimistic but precise prose and her stubborn insistence that things have feelings (*Your bunched-up stockings are insulted by their unjust treatment at your hands! Your coat appreciates a little thanks for keeping you warm every day!*), combined with her lifelong passion for total control over her environment, have a unique way of inciting a truly life-changing bout of cathartic junk-purging. It's not that things aren't important, it's that some things are incredibly important and other things are literal garbage, garbage that keeps you from appreciating your most treasured possessions. Kondo convinces us that we carry around these mountains of trash with us only because we've been tricked into feeling guilty about letting them go.

Advanced-level Kondo offers particularly exquisite peeks into the author's madness: She refers to tidying up as a "once-in-a-lifetime special event," endorses "treat[ing] your bras like royalty," and recommends covering stuffed animals' eyes so that they can't flash you accusatory looks from that Goodwill-bound bin by the front door. In other words, calling Kondo's infatuation with organizing a "love of tidying" is a bit like praising a tsunami for its unmatched passion for redesigning entire coastlines. It's a personality disorder in motion more than a lifestyle brand. Perversely, that only makes it all the more magical.

But maybe it takes a slightly unhinged person to reverse our decades of mindless consumption. Who else would dare suggest, "The basic rule for papers: Discard everything"? (Are they not required to keep tax records in Japan?) Who else would name a section of her book "Photos: Cherish who you are now"? Imagine Southwest Airlines changing their slogan from "Wanna get away?" to "What are you running from?"

Kondo has never seemed quite in step with the rest of humanity. (Regarding letters: "Rather than putting them directly into the recycle bin, it is more respectful to cover them in a paper bag first.") Yet her semi-unhinged belief in the supernatural wonder of things is part of what makes her prose so riveting. The fact that she's writing these odd, gorgeous snippets of poetry about sifting soulfully through your sock drawer is a big part of her appeal.

Yet as Marie Kondo becomes an internationally known guru—a few years ago I received an invitation to hear her speak in Los Angeles, where she was going to share "wisdom and practical information," presumably about, you know, *folding*—it's important to remember the shadow-message that lies just underneath Kondo's shiny veneer of prim optimism: We live in a world that wants us to replace the hundred bags of worthless stuff we just threw out with a hundred more bags of worthless stuff—not eventually, not next week, but today. Capitalism is exquisitely designed to remind us at every turn that not only is our happiness contingent on our ability to purchase more stuff, but our inability to do so makes our unhappiness all but guaranteed.

The poetic subtext that turned Marie Kondo into something akin to a globally recognized religious figure, the Dalai Lama of decluttering, is that we *don't* need more stuff. More, in fact, is a sickness. Kondo's message is, and always has been, that we should work with what we have instead.

—

That's a message that's surprisingly difficult to find anywhere else. What would it mean to read all of the books you own, for example, before you buy a new book? What kind of a pariah would give used items as gifts? What if you resolved never to buy another article of clothing, and to only wear the clothes you already own? None of this sounds socially feasible. It might seem quirky or eccentric at best, downright pathological at worst.

Nowhere do we see this more than with our children, for whom stuff is the ultimate celebratory gesture. At kids' birthday parties, bags of cheap plastic junk are handed out as the guests leave. Parents have recurring conversations about the difficulty of forcing their kids to get rid of trinkets and unused toys; then another party rolls around and they're disseminating worthless crap like everyone else. If you were to throw a party and tell the kids to "go outside and make mud pies," you would only embarrass your kids. Birthdays are for stuff. Celebrations bring more stuff. Every holiday revolves around stuff—giving it, receiving it.

Most of us don't model happiness in a vacuum of things. But at a time when our screens are never far from our faces, advertisements for more new stuff flash in the margins of our view most of the hours of the day, and our shared public spaces are almost without fail commercial spaces, creating fun and happiness or even just appreciating solitude and silence adds up to an important survival strategy.

What would it feel like to spend a day without stuff?

—

The modern, minimalist home, with its "White Dove" walls and its recessed speakers and its smart-home technology, might seem like the natural, more evolved landing point in the rise and fall of materialism. Yet while spending a massive amount of money to get rid of or hide all unsightly possessions might look like emancipation, that kind of a life creates its own anxieties. It's the free-floating neuroticism that springs from attempting to maintain a sleek, spare home but always falling short. Because even though we all tend to tell ourselves a story of why we fail—we are lazy, we are bad at cleaning, we don't have time—the truth is that a clutter-free existence exerts a constant pressure that's oppressive in its own way.

And as interior design standards have trickled down from luxury hotels to outdoor malls to retail spaces to mom-and-pop restaurants to your friend's house (that somehow feels like a cross between a luxury hotel and a *Dwell* spread, how does she do it?), as regular humans peruse design magazines and pin photos of their dream apartments and houses on their Pinterest boards, the ability to simply live with your regular old ramshackle not-very-designed, somewhat cluttered habitat becomes harder and harder. Somehow, you're supposed to inhabit a pristine museum instead.

And minimalism is no longer just for the very rich or the under-occupied. Your house can't merely be clean; it also must be empty. Clutter is a symbol of your weakness, a sign of an unsophisticated mind, a sign that you don't know what's cool, a sign that you are falling behind. Upper-crust decluttering has trickled down and rendered the clutter-embracing slobs of the world obsolete.

These are the sorts of unrealistic social pressures that keep the stock market on its perpetual upward march. The economy expands to infinity only if our desires and expectations expand proportionately. Standards must always be shifting like unsteady ground beneath our feet. The manufacturing of shame dictates that every mundane thing we do that is currently seen as Acceptable and Good will eventually be deemed Not Good Enough by the cultural marketplace.

But if we envision a life of perpetually staying up-to-date with the styles, the trends, the sounds, the smells, the looks—let's not even say "the ideas," since ideas have come to feel as onerous and beside the point as file cabinets or Rolodexes, when compared to memes or screenshots or tweets—we are committing to a life that is cluttered but also disposable, a life in which it becomes harder and harder to distinguish between passions and trivia. Whereas Kondo herself might be viewed as a kind of prophet embracing "joy" in all of its sparest forms, the decluttering movement, as it has been metabolized by our culture, makes it clear that you're only sloughing off unnecessary things so that the new trends and styles and sounds and smells can be purchased and absorbed into your environment and sloughed off in turn. Ideally you will swim up a stream of things for your entire life.

Figuring out how to sort our belongings might sound trivial at first, but it forms part of our guiding modern religion, one that binds us to lifestyles built around excess while failing to meet our most basic human needs. Not only do modern consumer choices rarely bring us long-term satisfaction, but they're exhausting. It takes a lot of energy to recognize which signifiers will place you in the dreadful almost-past with the know-nothings who aren't always moving forward, always casting off and acquiring more, always focused on what comes next.

—

If she weren't herself subsumed by the same high capitalist processes that doomed her to become the human equivalent of needless clutter, Marie Kondo had the potential to be a true prophet of this strangely dissatisfying age. Because her message, that your things shouldn't make you feel anxious or guilty or unnerved or uncomfortable, can't help but sound like a rare drop of truth in a sea of madness. After all, it's not just our stuff that's making us anxious. It's also the thousands of messages on our phones, hovering before our faces every day, asking us to react, like, follow, listen, comment, retweet, forward, join, enlist, consume. We are besieged by alerts. The soundtrack to our days is our phone's relentless ping, ping, ping.

Turning your phone off, turning your sound off, going offline—these things are viewed not just as antisocial but as irresponsible. A few years ago, I had an acquaintance inform me that I had a "texting problem" because I didn't drop everything and text back at any hour of the day. I tried to explain that I'm a writer, so I need several hours of uninterrupted silent time to do my job. But because I work from home, this was met with eye rolls. You *must* answer more quickly, was the response. Everyone present agreed. I had a problem. Waiting four hours is too long. You must not mute the constant pinging. You are on call to everyone at all times.

The digital clutter of our lives doesn't merely make us anxious, interrupting our train of thought and blocking us from longer periods of silence and the deeper thinking that can go with it. Our digital clutter redesigns our world around the temporary. Constant interruptions turn us into amnesiacs who are required to respond, reply, and react from moment to moment. This is why we have so little memory of what happened last week, let alone what happened last year or twenty years ago. We are constantly threatened with interruption, so we experience each moment as something that could easily be discounted, could easily be erased or subsumed by some more-important message. Our minds, in other words, are filled with the clutter of what comes next: messages and tweets and texts yet to be received. We live in a world of past and future clutter. We are boxed in. There is no space for where we are right now.

It's no wonder we've responded so enthusiastically to the message of minimalism. Our minds are so filthy with noise and anticipated interruptions. There is no way to just be here, now.

By imbuing objects with feelings (in keeping with the Shinto tradition), Kondo underscored the importance of the feelings that our objects evoke in us. But when we tune in to those feelings, something strange happens. We start to recognize not just the joy that things can spark, but the anxiety as well: My iPhone makes me worried that the school could call at any minute to tell me my daughter is sick or hurt. My FitBit reminds me that I haven't exercised yet. My laptop reminds me that a catastrophe could be unfolding somewhere in the world right now, but I won't know about it until I check the news.

Can I step away from this digital maw? Will my voice still matter if no one can hear it? Can silence feel more pressing and important than a ping? Instead of imagining the next text, the next tweet, the next Instagram post, the next flash of what my cousin did over spring break or what my neighbor ate for breakfast, what if I could imagine living in this moment, without wanting more? The question isn't whether or not your stuff sparks joy. The question is: Can you spark joy all by yourself? Do you remember how that feels?

—

My father's wallet sits in the top drawer of my desk. Every few months, I pull it out and look at his money: $26—a twenty (dated 1990), a five (1993), and a one (1988). When this cash was in my dad's wallet, he was fifty-six years old. Along with that $26, he had a retirement fund, several investment properties, a condo, a brand-new Lexus coupe, and a small piece of paper stuck to his dresser mirror on which he had scrawled a reminder, in black ballpoint pen: "All of heaven is within you."

When I take my dad's wallet out of my desk drawer and hold it in my hands, it brings me what the Japanese would call *mono no aware,* which translates literally as "the pathos of things" but means more broadly, "a melancholic awareness of the transience of existence." My father's wallet reminds me that nothing lasts. Just when you're starting to get comfortable, you disappear. And maybe only one or two of your things will seem important to someone else when you're gone.

That's sad, but it's also a reason to wake up to the enormity of the moment, to the unbelievable gift of being alive, right now. You don't need more than this. All of heaven is within you.

running on empty

arriet Daimler, the protagonist of Iris Owens's 1973 novel *After Claude,* has a knack for eviscerating self-satisfied urban types. After rolling her eyes at a slender girl passing a joint (" 'I'm wrecked,' she bragged, as though it took a special talent to get stoned"), Harriet utters a relatable prayer: "Lord, spare me these dimpled darlings who are always congratulating themselves for not having any thoughts or feelings."

Harriet might have given those dimpled darlings a little more credit. Floating through life unencumbered by thoughts or feelings is more challenging than you might imagine. As the tabloids have demonstrated for decades now, even those with untold cash reserves and limitless adoration from the masses can't tamp down their neuroses or their melancholy for too long. Empowered to sip champagne among half-naked nymphs beside glittering swimming pools, somehow these mortals still struggle mightily to keep their pesky thoughts and feelings from messing with their good lives.

Neuroticism in paradise is rarely explored in the luxury-focused narratives that have filled the small screen for the past five or six decades. Escapist fantasies, after all, rely on images of glamorous, leisurely living to transport us from our ordinary living rooms into a gorgeous world inhabited by shiny, beautiful people. From *The Love Boat* to *Dynasty* to *The O.C.* to *Ballers,* such fantasies hold a special place in our culture. But none can quite stack up to the happy-go-lucky, high-fiving men at the center of HBO's *Entourage,* that mid-aughts exercise in wishful thinking. Since the show made its debut in 2004, the mood of celebrity culture has shifted from adoration (*Vanity Fair* profiles, expanded Oscar coverage, *Cribs*) to contempt (unflattering paparazzi close-ups, Gawker Stalker maps) to indifference, and back to a kind of obsession (Kim Kardashian, Beyoncé, and the cult of Instagram). Through it all, Vince and his posse remained ever the same: cruising in their SUVs, sipping on their lattes, and conquering slick agency offices and bass-thumping nightclubs alike with the slouchy nonchalance of sophomores at a kegger.

Their obliviousness to the shifting cultural climate could be viewed as a testament to the joys of living in a well-financed, hermetically sealed bubble of comfort, though it's easier to suspect that these four men were just plain oblivious. How else did Vince (played by Adrian Grenier), Drama (Kevin Dillon), Eric (Kevin Connolly), and Turtle (Jerry Ferrara) dedicate most of their time to the pursuit of pleasure without appearing to take much pleasure in any of it? Some have referred to *Entourage* as a West Coast, male version of *Sex and the City,* but the differences between the two shows are more instructive than the similarities. Unlike the promiscuous epicureans of *Sex and the City*, who recounted each romantic dalliance as if it were a meal at a five-star restaurant, Vince and his boys treated sex with pretty strangers like fast-food takeout. For a bunch of guys who ogled more curvilinear flanks per episode than Gopher and Isaac did on an entire season of *The Love Boat*, these four were remarkably dispassionate about their primary hobby.

And far from sweating the sexual small stuff, in the manner of Carrie, Samantha, Miranda, and Charlotte (This guy still lives with his mother! This guy has too much back hair!), the *Entourage* crew successfully swatted away apprehension wherever they found it, abandoning reflection or insight for bong hits and marathon sessions with the Xbox. Year after year, the frat-boy wisdom they repeated to each other remained the same: Nothing—not a job, not a woman, and certainly not a sense of your wasted potential—is worth losing sleep over.

—

Despite its fabled excesses, Hollywood has a healthy track record of self-mockery. As portrayals of fallen stars go, though, it's tough to beat the bitter former silent-movie legend Norma Desmond (Gloria Swanson) of *Sunset Boulevard* or the delusional former child star Jane Hudson (Bette Davis) of *What Ever Happened to Baby Jane?* Both Norma and Baby Jane have a predilection for creating imaginary worlds out of thin air—exactly the sort of talent that starts to look less enviable once the cheering crowds stop cheering and wander off. In these Tinseltown self-satires, thoughts and feelings are a liability, fame is a deadly acid that scars the psyche beyond recognition, and no star is so bright that it won't eventually flame out spectacularly.

The character who perhaps most memorably embodies the perils of intelligence and sensitivity in Hollywood is one who doesn't inhabit Hollywood at all—played again by Bette Davis, this time as Margo Channing in *All About Eve*, which is set in the world of New York theater. Margo can't even appreciate her glory days, because she's too smart not to know that they're numbered. Unable to censor herself or ignore the brutal superficiality around her, Margo transforms from celebrated starlet to self-imploding black hole of ego-driven darkness over the course of two hours. All of the paparazzi-incited outbursts in the world can't approach the simmering contempt of Margo's announcement, at a party of wary onlookers: "Fasten your seat belts, it's going to be a bumpy night."

In each of these movies, Hollywood's humiliations transform once-exalted divas into paranoid monsters with a compulsion either to regain their former glory or to stop at nothing to destroy the ascendantly glorious. Imagine if Vinnie Chase had that kind of passion! Even when he finally succumbed to a drug-fueled downward spiral, it came off with all of the heaviness of an after-school special, with Vince in Scott Baio's stoner role. But then, part of what made each season of *Entourage* feel interchangeable with the next was the fact that the corrupting influence of stardom never had any cumulative effect on Vince (or on us, the audience). Like an eternal ingénue, Vince remained magically resistant to the ego-bloating aspects of Hollywood life, never feasting on the empty praise of adoring fans or fawning studio heads. Instead, he partook of the string-bikini-clad spoils of fame with a casual levity. His one brief explosion of expletives and anger didn't feel motivated by anything as heavy as existential dread or a wounded ego. He was just a little peeved that night, too low on sleep and not high enough on coke to make small talk with strangers.

Of course, the top priority of *Entourage* was always to keep

Vince likable enough that the show's vicarious celebrity thrills might remain intact. Daring to make Vince needy or self-involved or occasionally bombastic, daring to make him legitimately resentful of the so-called compadres who latched onto him, socially and financially, with the tenacity of a stubborn fungal infection, would go against the show's lighthearted, "it's all good" tone.

Against a backdrop of endlessly thumping beats and endlessly circling babes, all of which felt pretty *meh* by the end of the show's run, a day of reckoning would've made perfect sense. But no day of reckoning ever came. In the show's final season, we rejoined a clean and sober Vince cheerfully attending N.A. meetings, and his boys were soon back to sipping from bottles of Budweiser. Instead of serving as either cautionary tale (*All About Eve*) or upper-class urban fairy tale (*Sex and the City*), *Entourage* was just a story about some guys with a knack for making sex, drugs, and rock 'n' roll look remarkably lackluster, as their repetitive banter blended into a muddled white noise of macho, mutual white-people ribbing.

Each supporting character got to have exactly one emotional state: Drama's insecurity; Eric's lukewarm interest in marrying his girlfriend, Sloan; and Turtle's vague desire to build a career (preferably one that involves lots of deal-making on private jets). Beyond that, the guys rarely rose a few heartbeats above flatlining. It's no wonder that the only character on the show who truly engaged its audience was the superagent Ari Gold (Jeremy Piven). Ari was part mastermind and part buffoon—aggressive, offensive, and constantly ashamed. In other words, he was the sort of conflicted character who would feel perfectly at home in a classic tale of Hollywood corruption like *The Bad and the Beautiful*. Unlike Vince and his cadre of fools, Ari thought big thoughts, felt big feelings, and made one big mistake after another, while the others—Vince, Drama, Turtle,

Eric—shuffled across polished floors with the superficial self-assurance of men so insulated from the real world that they couldn't really remember what mediocre sushi tasted like.

—

When you watch a few episodes of *Entourage* in a row, with its relentless quips between bromantic heroes, gazing blankly at strippers rotating endlessly like fatted calves on spits, you start to feel a bit like Johnny Marco, the disaffected hero of a very different snapshot of the celebrity life: Sofia Coppola's transfixing film *Somewhere*. Living in the Chateau Marmont's celebrity playpen, escorted from one promotional appearance to the next, Johnny (Stephen Dorff) slowly loses his ability to feel any semblance of joy or excitement. Johnny—and Vince, in his own breezy way—represented a modern analog to the classic Hollywood parable about the corrupting influence of stardom. But instead of clinging to his fame and fortune like those divas of yore, Johnny relinquished his humanity to it. In the film's most haunting scene, Johnny's head is encased in white plaster for a role. We sit for several uncomfortable minutes in a quiet room with this faceless Nowhere Man, listening to him struggle to control his breathing. Even as his true self is erased for the sake of commodity, those thoughts and feelings still pound inside his rib cage, demanding to be heard. Of course, you have to have thoughts and feelings for that to happen. The boys of *Entourage* never convinced us that they do.

That's because *Entourage* was purposefully designed as an extreme male fantasy of ignorant bliss—a state that, in real life, can be tough to attain without the aid of narcotics. Even though these four men were demeaned repeatedly—Turtle by Vince's hot leftovers, Drama by the industry, Vince by women who were always smarter than he was, and Eric by pretty much everyone—somehow they always managed to shrug it off over a few cold ones. Like Iris Owens's dimpled darlings, they congratulated themselves (and each other) with high-fives and backslaps every time one of them returned to what they saw as their one true calling: mindless *hanging out*. And it's true, their talent for maintaining such a void of thoughts and feelings *was* pretty exceptional. But it also explains why there is no *Entourage*-themed corollary to that game where you name which *Sex and the City* character you are. The answer is always "Vince." Because no one wants to be those other guys.

—

Escapist fantasies have changed venues since the peak of *Entourage:* The posh life has migrated from the relative remove of TV shows and glossy celebrity lifestyle magazines to the intimacy of Instagram accounts. A window into the unimaginable lifestyles of the super-rich now lives in our pockets. Luxury feels more immediate and more attainable than it ever has before—and this makes it all the more unnerving.

There is also less acknowledgment now that these glimpses into rarefied worlds constitute escapist indulgences. No longer framed as guilty pleasures aimed at distracting us momentarily, the luxury of Instagram is so integrated into our lives that it's hard not to experience a regular, low-level sensation of injustice from it. Instagram feels designed to incite dissatisfaction. But not only that: We *all* feel like we deserve luxury now.

In fact, images of other people's experiences dominate so much of our own lives that we sometimes forget to wonder how it actually feels to live inside of those images. We are trained to care only about how good they look. Each shiny photograph holds the same message: "This woman looks better than you and she #wokeuplikethis." Or: "This guy's world is more beautiful and expensive than your world." Like Vince and his friends, we are not invited to peruse other people's real thoughts or feelings. We are invited to imagine a beautiful, blissful place where thoughts or feelings no longer exist.

This state of nothingness is the ultimate luxury. Freed from the cages of our minds and our physical desires, we might finally take in the glory of that sparkling pool, those circling girls. We might finally attain Vince's ideal of effortless, easy-going emptiness.

But these kinds of desires can only live in images. Because we can't be at the center of the party, listening to the hottest track, surrounded by slow-motion dancing babes. In real life, someone is always yelling over the music and ruining the whole song. The track skips just when it was getting good. Someone has cilantro stuck in her teeth. Reality is, by nature, disappointing. Thoughts and feelings almost always get in the way of pure luxury, as it is currently understood. Because luxury is at once intimate (via Chrissy Teigen's Instagram feed) and hard to feel these days. You can't live there. But somehow you can't stop peeking in the window like a stalker, either.

The other day, I found myself getting lost in a photo of Kim Kardashian and Kanye West. The picture was taken on Sunday morning. They were wearing the Kardashian-Kanye version of their Sunday Best, standing next to a white wall, on a pristine beige floor. I found myself wondering what kind of unholy army of stylists and maids and nannies and fluffers it took to paint and smooth and primp them into this flawless, serene state. Were the kids screaming right before the photo was taken, because the maids and the stylists and the nannies were circling too quickly and it was jacking with their nerves? Did the kids pull Kim's hair out of place? Was Kanye complaining about this need to photograph every minute of their lives? "It's Easter," Kanye tells Kim. "This is what I *do*," Kim replies. "This is my brand. Why do I have to justify it every few minutes? This is what keeps the lights on. This is what waters the enormous lawn outside."

Kanye sighs. Why does she have to mention the lawn? All of that beautiful grass makes him feel lonely for some reason, as if he lives in Central Park but everyone else is dead. His throat hurts. He's catching another cold. Too much flying. "I want us to be normal for a second," he tells her. "Is that—can you just . . . ?"

"What's normal?" Kim asks.

—

The Fyre Festival in the spring of 2017 marked the crowning disaster of mass-marketed luxury, exemplifying the growing gap between image and reality. Trailers circulated online to promote the festival showed the requisite overtanned, plump-assed models in butt floss, swimming through crystal blue waters of the Caribbean, riding on Jet Skis, interspersed with shadowy footage of a crowded concert where everyone is feeling the love, feeling the beat, feeling the liquor, just feeling it. Imagine feeling the same thing that everyone else is feeling. No thinking is involved; you are perfectly in sync with the music and the crowd.

But this was *footage* of feeling it, which is different from actually feeling it. And as ticket holders to the Fyre Festival discovered when they arrived in the Bahamas, having been promised great music, luxury accommodations, and five-star chefs, previews of the Fyre Festival turned out to be a universe apart from the actual Fyre Festival. What they found, instead of supermodels frolicking to sick beats in paradise, were falling-over disaster relief tents and biting flies and cold cheese sandwiches, served on a scrubby beach.

And unlike the mythical visions of luxury held up by Instagram, once this new footage emerged it was all too easy to imagine exactly how it felt to attend the *real* Fyre Festival. Anyone could conjure the feeling of sitting on a folding chair in the sand on an overcast day, surrounded by swirling flies, staring at a slice of processed cheese sweating in the heat. "I paid ten thousand dollars for VIP access," said a moist-looking young man waiting at an overheated airport in one of the videos. The wavering of his voice told us he was bewildered by his fate. "How do things like this even happen?" his sad eyes beseeched us.

But this is what the real-life luxury often feels like: disappointment. Why are these luxury towels so scratchy? Why is this luxury sky so gray? Why is this luxury cocktail so overly sweet and devoid of alcohol? Where is my luxury waiter, and why is this luxury steak he brought me so overcooked? Why are these not-very-luxurious, loud-talking people here in paradise with me, acting not all that luxuriously like they own paradise just as much as I do?

In fact, believing that you belong in paradise—and that paradise will somehow feel as good as a picture of paradise looks—has a way of emptying out the joys of paradise pretty rapidly. That's why *Entourage* felt like such a crime against humanity, even on those rare occasions when we were able to savor its vicarious thrills: It was impossible not to recognize how Vinnie and the boys' entitlement and arrogance only made the tedium of cruising through the same scantily clad crowds at pool parties over and over again all the more insufferable. It was tough not to long for Margo Channing, seething and spitting at the pretense and emptiness of it all.

Instead of striving for a life that could somehow match the clean beauty of an image from Instagram or the blurry glory of a trailer for an orgiastically great concert that could never happen, imagine striving for a way to encounter the small details of everyday life as if they were unexpectedly delightful. Isn't that how luxury is supposed to feel, after all? Luxury means being able to relax and savor the moment, knowing that it doesn't get any better than this.

Feeling that way doesn't require money. It doesn't require the perfect scenery. All that's required is an ability to survey a landscape that is disheveled, that is off-kilter, that is slightly unattractive or unsettling, and say to yourself: *This is exactly how it should be.* This requires a big shift in perspective: Since your thoughts and feelings can't simply be turned off, you have to train your thoughts and feelings to experience imperfections as acceptable or preferable—even divine.

The sky is gray. A fly lands on your hand. Your cocktail is lukewarm. And still, for some reason, if you slow down and accept reality enough, it starts to feel right. Better than right. You are not comparing reality to some imagined perfect alternative. You are welcoming reality for what it already is.

And what if you have no cocktail, because you're sober now? And what if your neck is aching? Maybe you're running late. Maybe you feel anxious. Still, you pay attention to each little fold, each disappointment, each impatient attempt by mind and body to "fix" what already is. And then surrender to all of it. These details are irreplaceable. They give the moment its value. The chance to soak in this mundane, uneven moment is the purest luxury of all.

lost treasure

When I was about ten years old, I sometimes visited an elderly widow named Indye who lived in a little house around the corner from ours. She would serve me some stale vanilla Hydrox cookies and a little Dixie cup of grape juice and then she'd show me her "arrangements," crafts she'd glued together from mostly natural materials: a smooth piece of driftwood with tiny dried flowers and a curled bit of dried kudzu vine glued to it, or an oblong stone with a patch of moss and a small arching branch over it. She had dozens of these creations to share with me at any given time. She'd spend a solid two or three minutes describing each one to me, how she'd found the driftwood on a beach trip with her sister (who lived next door), how she'd noticed the curled kudzu vine on a recent walk, along with a really beautiful piece of bark with moss growing out of its cracks. "Now, Heathuh," she'd say in her posh Virginian accent, resting one old hand on my arm and gesturing with her other hand, "what do you think of *this* one?"

I was a polite kid, so I would try to sound enthusiastic ("I like it a lot," "It's pretty!"), nodding along and asking questions and oooing and ahhing over her discoveries. But the whole exercise was pretty exhausting. The pace was just so *slow*. Standing for so long like that on her immaculate white carpet, watching her old hands gesture at each conglomeration of twigs and flowers and moss lined up neatly on her credenza—it felt absolutely excruciating to me. She would say a few words ("Now *this* one, Heathuh . . ."), then stop to reach for a tissue out of her pocket, to dab at her perpetually watery eyes and her perpetually drippy nose. Then she'd say, "Well, now, my alluhgies are acting up again, isn't that *awwwful?*" and I'd nod, but I suspected that old people just leaked all the time. And anyway, it probably didn't help your allergies to drag so many weedy and twiggy things home with you around the clock. Then my mind would wander to the many, many things I'd rather be doing than standing in this chilly overly air-conditioned house, with its shutters drawn tight against the sunshine, talking about these tiny bits of glued-together junk.

"One man's trash is anothuh man's treashuh!" Indye would exclaim, as if reading my mind. She didn't have any grandchildren and her husband had died a decade earlier. She told me one day that she was eighty-three years old, whispered it to me after a lot of dramatic fanfare about a "big secret," and then she made me promise not to tell a soul. Later I found out that she told my sister and my mom the same secret. "One man's trash is anothuh man's treashuh!" my mom would sometimes declare out of the blue, and then laugh. But my mom thought

Indye was smart and interesting. Indye's sister and her sister's husband were nice people, but Indye was eccentric. My mom liked eccentric more than she liked nice.

I did feel pretty virtuous at the end of each visit, knowing that I'd done my duty and given our lonely neighbor a little company. "Now, Heathuh. Which of my arrangements do you think is your favorite?" she'd ask. I knew she was going to give me whichever one I chose, and I didn't really want to take anything that she should keep and sell at one of her craft fairs instead, but I didn't want to insult her by refusing.

Maybe she shouldn't have given up one of her best creations to a kid. I probably put it on my shelf and shuffled it around and eventually it might've ended up in a toy bin somewhere, falling apart. (One man's treashuh is anothuh man's trash.) My mother, at least, put the arrangements Indye gave her behind glass, next to her art books.

———

It all sounds downright exotic to me now, the thought of going on long walks and paying enough attention that you might notice a bit of interesting bark or a slim reed or curled vine. Imagine that kind of slow focus, combing the woods or the beach for something to work with.

When I go on walks these days, I listen to podcasts and answer texts and make phone calls. I listen to Kendrick Lamar, who is grateful but also pissed off. That's my territory: gratitude and anger, anger and gratitude. It's an impatient place to live. I don't silently scan the sidewalk for interesting twigs or leaves or bottle caps. I pick up my dog's shit and wonder what bad news I'm missing. I cough and sneeze because my allergies are acting up. (Allergies aren't just an excuse for rheumy old-person eyes, as it turns out.) I read texts that say things like, "Happy Mother's Day to a bunch of amazing moms!" and I think "I would not personally classify my mothering as amazing." But I still spend at least a block texting back "Have a great day!" with multiple heart emojis. It's odd to send heart emojis when your heart feels not particularly warm, when your distracted brain is too preoccupied with the news and allergies and dog shit to focus on love and motherhood and being amazing.

It's hard to live in the moment, to exist locally and think locally and emote locally. Something in my pocket is always buzzing. People far away expect quick answers to every passing question. Why do we live this way?

Imagine, instead, a day of quiet wandering. Imagine tuning in to what's around you, instead of getting distracted by events and sounds and messages that have nothing to do with where you are. Imagine taking some time to notice the wind in the leaves, the sunshine on the grass, the smallest seedpod drifting through the air, the oddly shaped stone resting at the edge of the creek. Indye's hobby wasn't just gluing junk together. Her hobby was the search itself. Every day's walk held new promise.

I didn't see Indye after I left home for college, and I always thought that she died a few years later. But the other day I looked up her obituary online, and it turns out she lived to be 105 years, eight months, and fifteen days old. I wonder if she kept looking for new treasures for years after I knew her. I wonder if she kept whispering her secret into new ears for another two decades.

The future turned out to be just as incredible as I imagined it would be when I was little. But these days, I just want to slow down. I want to pull the shutters closed and block out the world. I want to spend hours gluing things together. I want to fill my house with tiny bits of collected junk. The more I have, the more I realize that all that matters is the small discoveries, the little interactions, the improvised, messy, glued-together moments that lie at the center of our happiness. Everything else is just a distraction.

the land of heroic villains

The premise of *The Sopranos* was simple: A mob boss begins therapy. Tony Soprano was a bad guy who did bad things, but he was conflicted about it. *Why* did he do bad things? Well, he couldn't afford the mortgage to his big house in New Jersey if he stopped doing bad things. He'd have to make all new friends. He'd also have to avoid getting shot in the head by his former associates, then pushed off a boat with a bag of rocks tied to his feet.

When the show premiered on HBO in 1999, it was unusual to cast a criminal as your leading man. But as strange as it was to root for a bad guy, we did it. Something about Tony's regular life in the suburbs made it possible. We even felt a little sorry for him. Pop psychology had yet to overrun our world, transforming celebrity interviews and song lyrics and Prius jingles alike into a mélange of dime-store psychoanalysis and interrogate-your-deepest-self psychobabble. But even if probing the psychic depths of complete strangers wasn't yet common practice, we recognized that Tony's mother was mean to him, that Tony's wife, Carmela, acted holier than thou, even though she didn't *really* want Tony to leave the mob, because that would mean she'd lose the mansion and the Porsche Cayenne and the designer handbags.

We also saw that Tony truly cared about his wife and his kids, in his own awkward, sexist, clumsy-bear-paws-hugging-you-too-hard kind of way. From some angles, Tony was a big softy: He was sentimental about the ducks that came to swim in his pool. He felt depressed about getting old. He worried about dying—that he'd drop dead of a heart attack one day and nothing he'd done would matter. When Tony went to therapy and told Dr. Melfi his darkest fears, we didn't identify, but we empathized.

Nonetheless, *Sopranos* creator David Chase never wanted us to forget that his protagonist was a thug, plain and simple. Tony and his cohorts Silvio and Big Pussy and Christopher were the worst sorts of people: ignorant, reckless, amoral. It wasn't just that they were insatiable and easily bored and lacked any kind of a moral compass. These people were capable of careless acts of unspeakable cruelty. They could put down their sandwiches to kill someone, and then finish their sandwiches afterward. They could interrupt an argument to kill someone, then continue arguing. They killed their close friend Big Pussy; then Silvio calmly removed Big Pussy's watch and jewelry and kept it before they threw his body overboard.

In other words, audiences may have come to empathize with Tony Soprano over the years, but David Chase never did. Tony rarely learned anything worthwhile in therapy. He never made progress. Everything he wanted, he wanted for himself alone. He often grew enraged at his therapist, Dr. Melfi, just for seeing him so clearly. He resented her intelligence. He resented her power over him. He tried to experience things like gratitude and generosity, but his selfishness, his rage, his greed, and his laziness always got in the way.

The true irony of *The Sopranos*—the show that gave rise to our so-called golden age of television, that inspired countless TV heroes who were, by any honest estimation, reprehensible villains—was that, though Chase aimed to subvert the black and white morality of most TV dramas, his creation wound up as a morality play. As intrigued as we were by these men who committed evil acts, we weren't supposed to unabashedly embrace them.

But we did anyway. Viewers forgave Tony. They embraced Tony and Carmela and Christopher as if they were members of their own family. In forums and comments sections in 2010, the year the show wrapped, fans worried loudly about the fate of these beloved characters: They not only wanted Tony to evade prison and survive, but they wanted him to live happily ever after. They posted romantic videos of Tony and Carm's best moments—as if he'd never hit her, as if she never called him a cheating bastard, as if they were the sweet married couple who lived next door.

Chase knew that if he killed Tony, he'd make a martyr of the character. Prison was also too good for Tony. The show's finale, in its abruptness and lack of conclusion, suggested that Chase wanted Tony to suffer for all eternity instead, stuffing his face with onion rings while scanning the entrances and exits for a would-be assassin. He wanted Tony to be seared into our memories exactly the way he'd lived: indulging but insatiable, wallowing in nostalgia, trying to show his kids love but finding fault with them instead, trying to enjoy the moment but being too distracted, too jittery, too afraid, too anxious to be present. There would be no peaceful rest for Tony, no sentimental denouement. Tony would disappear without redemption and without fanfare, as deeply corrupt and irreparably broken as America itself.

The series finale almost felt like a rebuke to the show's Tony-loving fans. Its conclusion suggested that even when your evil acts aren't punished, living such a deeply selfish life brings no joy, no lasting satisfaction, no happy ending. In an episode that was widely resented for its abrupt cut to a black screen at the end, Chase may have gone one step further, implicating not just Tony but also those who loved and embraced him. In that final scene, Chase seemed to be telling us that if all we want to do is shuffle along in a haze of nostalgia, seeking an endless stream of indulgences and distractions, we weren't much better than Tony himself. Tony (who murdered people in cold blood) was not much worse than Carmela (who benefited from Tony's corruption), who was about as bad as most of us (who benefit from our country's corruption, living lives of privilege as the poor continue to suffer). A life without values, in other words, is a life without meaning. Or as Tony's mother, Livia Soprano, once put it, "It's all a big nothing."

—

If *The Sopranos* represents an early-aughts litmus test of American moral relativism (a slope that arguably began slipping the moment Pilgrims set foot on American soil), Showtime's *Billions* represents the unquestioned peak of our willingness to indulge patriarchal corruption. The show, which premiered in 2016, centers on Bobby Axelrod, a hedge fund titan with a penchant for striding down glass-walled corridors while spitting out one-liners abrasive enough to make Gordon Gekko blush. Axelrod (played by Damien Lewis) is the very definition of bravado unbounded by any moral compass. "When I pull a deal off the table, I leave Nagasaki behind!" he growls at one point, demonstrating his habit of conflating senseless brutality with power. In promotions for the show, HBO repeated the same clip over and over of Axelrod's face in close-up, saying with a sneer, "What's the use of Fuck You Money if you never say 'fuck you'?" The clip embodied the macho premise of the show itself: Why get rich if you can't screw someone over and then rub their face in it? Isn't that the whole point of being wealthy?

Up until *Billions,* the villainous leading men of premium cable tended to land in their morally questionable circumstances under duress. Walter White was broke and dying of cancer when he turned to making and selling meth on *Breaking Bad.* Vic Mackey of *The Shield* was a dirty cop not because he was evil, but because the bureaucracy of lawful policing left too many bad guys on the streets, plus his kid had autism that required therapy beyond the reach of a cop's salary. Breaking the rules in this context—messing up people's lives, hurting innocent bystanders—was collateral damage in the battle for survival. In contrast, on *Billions,* unethical moves aren't some unfortunate side effect, they're the characters' entire raison d'être. Axelrod, along with his associates and his nemesis, Attorney General Chuck Rhoades (played by Paul Giamatti), aren't attempting to right wrongs or bend rules because they have no choice. They simply want to win at any cost. They're proud of any behavior, moral or not, that leads to victory.

Victory is not enough, of course. These guys want to win while everyone else loses; otherwise it's not as fun. What's the joy in flying first class if there aren't any poor slobs in the rows behind you? Every bit of dialogue, every monologue, every passing remark emphasizes riding high at the expense of someone else's misery. In every scene, these men plan new ways to take each other down.

In keeping with the trope of the premium drama, Bobby Axelrod sees a therapist, as Tony Soprano did. But he doesn't talk about his feelings in order to know himself better or to feel his feelings more deeply. His therapist—or "performance coach," as they call it at his firm—is there to help him win more effectively. Axelrod and his employees only explore their emotions in order to gain control over them. Feelings, like competitors or financial regulators or moral codes, are merely obstacles to success.

Remorse sometimes rears its head in *Billions*: Axelrod realizes that he ruined the lives of a few non-enemies along the way, a fact he's not proud of. Rhoades messes up his marriage by being a ruthless dick. But these moments don't come back to haunt them. There are no recurring nightmares, like the ones that plagued Tony. Axelrod and Rhoades don't care enough about other people's feelings to be unnerved by them.

The underlying premise of *Billions* has nothing to do with regret—and it has, somewhat ironically, little to do with money. Axelrod's life looks pretty joyless. Absent, too, is the melancholy or dissatisfaction of Tony Soprano. Where Soprano often gave the impression of craving more—more love, more power, more sex, more pasta—Axelrod only wants to roam the glistening halls of his hedge fund offices, master of his domain, restless but in command.

Billions is a voyeuristic exercise in which we imagine the accumulation of money, power, influence, and vengeance in fast motion. Who will be humiliated? Who will reign supreme? We aren't supposed to consider the long-term side effects of such a life. We are to delight in the brutal clash of wills. To ask whether it's ethical or base, healthy or destructive, worthwhile or worthless, is to miss the point entirely.

—

The operating system that guides *Billions* reflects the culmina-
tion of years of cultural programming that either savors the
gray area of any moral puzzle or else sidesteps the issue of
morality altogether. But TV comedies are in many ways even
more depraved than dramas. Where Woody Allen may have
taken us down the path of the lazy and entitled, he tended
to treat his characters' indiscretions as the outgrowth of any
sophisticated adult male's natural desires, thereby sidestepping
moral dilemmas the second they arose. ("Of course we'd all
like to sleep with teenagers instead of our wives," he suggested
with a wink, as if this admission made him adorably raffish
and not a criminal.) *Seinfeld*'s morality went deeper, acknowledging that being an intelligent, entitled New Yorker doesn't
exempt you from being judged as repugnant. The show demonstrated over and over again that selfish, lazy people can
do actual, concrete harm, even if they don't necessarily lose
sleep over the consequences of their actions. (Remember when
George's fiancé died from licking the cheap envelopes he
bought for their wedding invitations?)

Most of our "golden age" comedies, from *Curb Your
Enthusiasm* to *Veep* to the works of Judd Apatow, follow in
this Seinfeldian tradition. The characters are self-serving and
pathetic and unscrupulous; that's what makes them funny.
In dramedies like *Weeds, Transparent, Fleabag,* and *Big Little Lies,* selfish, myopic, pathetic behaviors are treated as the
most entertaining aspects of privileged people. Indeed television has been marinating in blatant, unpunished selfishness
for long enough now, in our scripted programming but also
in our nightly news, that it's as though we're slipping back
into Woody Allen territory. The shores of our morality recede,
but the tide of forgiveness rises to meet it. In such a world, of
course you'd sleep with your best friend's ex-boyfriend. Stealing from your family, selling drugs, cheating on your husband—

these things "just happen," requiring little explanation or apology. We all make mistakes.

American exceptionalism, which always included some talk of bravery and honor but also privileged winners over losers and haves over have-nots, may have finally curdled into this craven survivalist brutality. TV reflects our culture's fundamentalist roots leavened by an almost surreal disentanglement from our long-held standards of behavior. It's not just a void of ethics that we're witnessing, though; it's the celebration of that void. Many of our most popular narratives sidestep unwieldy talk of values, a seemingly outmoded term, in favor of a recurring struggle to dominate, or else to avoid domination. Brutality, mercilessness, lack of concern for principles—these are painted as prerequisites. In a 2017 interview with *The Guardian*, British documentary filmmaker Louis Theroux remarked on the U.S. president, "Trump saw through so much. For all his awfulness, I can't but help admire his shamelessness, in an odd way. Or maybe not admire, but be fascinated by it and maybe envy it. In a shame culture he seems to have figured out that if you refuse to be shamed, it gives you enormous power."

In other words, power is admirable no matter the source. If being terrible makes it possible to win, then it makes perfect sense to be terrible. Terribleness itself becomes admirable.

More than just our triumphant, pioneering spirit, or the heroes we made of the robber barons of the Gilded Age, perhaps it's America's long embrace of rebellion that should answer for our current moment. Because no culture has conflated knee-jerk defiance with heroic independence and tenacity quite like America has, from John Wayne to Marlon Brando to James Dean to Elvis to Fonzie. We've metabolized decades of stories in which the day must always be saved by a renegade who exists above the law. The heroes of our dramas, movies, reality TV—and now our celebrities and political leaders—share a lack of respect for traditional limits guiding their behavior. Rules are there merely to be broken.

But there's also something oddly outdated in this thinking, as authoritarian corruption becomes commonplace. When Bobby Axelrod pulls off his oxford shirt and replaces it with a black Megadeth T-shirt before a meeting with Chuck Rhoades, we're supposed to think, admiringly, "This guy truly gives zero fucks." The show's creators may have misjudged the moment. Because instead of looking cool, Axelrod just looks like a prematurely old man, one whose worldview is expiring before his eyes.

—

It's not hard to chart America's moral decline in retrospect, just by examining our cultural artifacts. But many of us didn't realize until 2017 that the self-serving villains and sociopaths on our screens also populated our real-life offices and schools and neighborhoods. And if producer Harvey Weinstein's long history of sexual harassment had been exposed in 1997 instead of 2017, it might've felt like the fulfillment of a cliché. The studio head who demands head in exchange for a plum role was such an accepted part of the entertainment industry narrative (and its sickness) for so long that it was a running joke. That's certainly how his onetime lawyer Lisa Bloom tried to frame it, referring to Weinstein as "an old dinosaur trying to learn new ways."

But in 2017, it felt as if an increasingly grotesque subspecies of infantile beast had escaped the screen and invaded our real lives. Suddenly, we found ourselves wondering: Does the world even feel real to powerful men? How else do two world leaders with nuclear weapons capable of murdering millions trade juvenile insults on Twitter like kids battling over a video game? What else makes it seem tempting to break a window in a hotel tower and point one of forty-three assault weapons at a crowd below, as Stephen Paddock did in Las Vegas in October 2017, killing fifty-eight people before turning the gun on himself? And unbelievably enough, no one seemed prepared to take action to prevent more harm. Were we really going to hold our collective breaths and watch these angry men determine our fates? How was this reality?

Lisa Bloom had misjudged the moment the same way the writers of *Billions* had. Even before the full extent of his crimes emerged, we couldn't see Weinstein as a friendly dinosaur, or take the faux-humble words of his apology seriously. "Though I'm trying to do better," he wrote, "I know I have a long way to go." It seemed absurd that we were meant to picture a sad, endangered brute brought low and forced to reflect on his sins closely for the first time, and not, say, a guy who had been paying women to stay quiet for over three decades.

The whole picture was so perplexing. Why did Weinstein so often insist that employees and actresses meet him in his hotel room, opening his robe to reveal his naked body to them like some kind of a sick surprise? Did their repulsion remind him of his power? Did it feel useless to have so much power if he couldn't lord it over a woman, and make her feel small and powerless by comparison?

When you really slow down the tape on Weinstein—or Donald Trump, or Bill Cosby, or Bill O'Reilly, or Roger Ailes—what you see more than anything else is a profound lack of connection to other human beings. It's not *just* that women, or strangers, or people of color, or children of immigrants, or Muslims (or a combination thereof), don't rate in their world. It's that these people are utterly irrelevant. A person is either useful and part of the club, or else that person is cast out like trash. The second someone ceases to be useful, they are forgotten. No big deal, time to finish your sandwich.

Harvey Weinstein's trail of victims allows us to appreciate the collateral damage of those monsters we, too, readily glorified on our screens. By sympathizing with a steady flow of merciless men, we've unwittingly transformed our shared notion of what makes a man powerful, what makes a man admirable, what makes a man truly free. It's tempting to believe that we can live inside this illusion, and blot the victims out of sight when their presence becomes inconvenient or uncomfortable for us. It's tempting to believe that there will be no cost to our recklessness and our abandonment of principle. It's easier not to worry about these things. But the dark truth of what we've been avoiding for years now seems to be rising before our eyes. The fantasy world we created, in which villains triumph and are lauded as heroes, slowly led us to a new, nightmarish reality. But unlike our fictional villains, we will be forced to reckon with our sins, whether we want to or not.

the popularity contest

ately I keep thinking about the Count, the puppet from the 1970s educational kids' show *Sesame Street*. He looked like Count Dracula, but he didn't want to suck your blood. All he wanted was to count things. This made him something of a social pariah. He couldn't make small talk. He never asked anyone about their day. All he cared about was numbers. If you tried to introduce him to your kids, he'd ignore their names and yell "ONE CHILD, TWO CHILDREN!"

He seemed cheerful, but he couldn't focus. He was constantly distracted by counting. His head was full of numbers. His whole life was passing him by, but he didn't notice. Numbers were everything to him. There was nothing else.

I know the feeling. These days, most of us offer up pieces of ourselves online—photos of our dogs, links to articles we read, opinions, jokes, announcements about future events, memes, clever turns of phrase—and they're translated into a number. Their value is quantified and they're emptied of meaning. All we have are the numbers: likes, retweets, more followers, fewer followers. Everything we have to offer is assigned a number. The number tells us how popular we are, and how popular our thoughts and experiences and opinions are.

What amazes me is how thoroughly this filter of numbers has invaded my worldview and the worldviews of those around me. I am asked to give a signal boost to almost every creative person I know, because my identifying Twitter number seems high enough that I could make a small difference. My number is privilege. I can tweet something stupid and a few people will like it, despite the fact that it's stupid. My number means I am seen. I am not being ignored. There is hope among professionals whose fortunes are linked to mine that my number will continue to grow, and my endeavors will continue to succeed.

My number provides the dangerous illusion that there's a crowd waiting to hear my next thought. (A small crowd, though I was told by a publicist that my number includes an "alarming percentage of influencers," which made me feel proud of myself, but in an empty way that left a strange, sour aftertaste.) The whole experience feels tempting and seductive and also stupid and embarrassing. But a small percentage of my acquaintances value these things, and they lament that their number is too low, and they ask me how I do it, even though my number isn't that impressive. I sometimes enjoy the fact that they feel tortured by this, possibly because I'm a bad person.

So how *do* I do it? What is my trick?

My trick is that I'm sometimes willing to interrupt real-life interactions with real people in order to stare at imaginary numbers instead. I tell myself I'm just filling my time with something fun. I tell myself that this is how I stay on top of the latest news. I tell myself that I work hard and I deserve an empty distraction.

Even though I'm not obsessed with status in general, for some messed-up reason I do like to look at these numbers. I enjoy the illusion of a waiting audience. It makes me feel less invisible and irrelevant, and those are maybe the saddest, stupidest words I've ever written.

I often seem cheerful, but I can't focus. I'm constantly distracted by my numbers. And sometimes it feels like I'm slowly going crazy along with all of the other ambivalent puppet people of social media. Our whole lives are passing us by, but we hardly notice. We are emptying out everything in our lives in exchange for meaningless figures on a screen. We are disappearing in plain sight.

—

For four years as *The Cut*'s "Ask Polly" columnist, and for years before that on my blog and elsewhere, I've fielded letters from young people looking for advice. I've noticed certain themes coming up over and over again, so much so that lately, I'm starting to believe that many of our basic assumptions about millennials—that they're spoiled and entitled, that they're overconfident in their abilities, that they're digital natives utterly unconflicted about privacy and social media and living much of their lives online—are wrong. What I discover in my email in-box each morning are dispatches from young people who feel guilty and inadequate at every turn and who compare themselves relentlessly to others. They are turned inside out, day after day, by social media. From my vantage point, it looks tougher to be a young person today than it has been for decades.

Of course, I'm dealing with a small, demographically skewed sample (though no more so, probably, than our "millennial" stereotype, so skewed toward the affluent and white). And my sample is self-selecting, too; I hear mostly from those who are struggling. Even so, their testimonies are heartwrenching. The same words and phrases and expressions of self-consciousness and self-doubt show up in letter after letter: "I often feel overwhelmingly middle ground or average in [my coworkers'] eyes," one writer confesses. Another asks, "When is he going to realize that I am an anxious mess who overthinks everything and hates herself, like, a lot of the time?" "I think my primary emotion is guilt," another writes. "When I am happy, it only takes moments before I feel guilty about it—I feel desperately unworthy of my happiness, guilty for receiving it out of the pure chaotic luck of the universe."

Many of these anxieties take the same shape: An external mob is watching and judging and withholding approval. It's impossible to matter, to be interesting enough. Many young people describe others as "a better version of me." This is how it feels today to be young and fully invested in our new popularity contest: No matter how hard you try, someone else out there is taking the same raw ingredients and making a better life out of them. The curated version of you that lives online also feels hopelessly polished and inaccurate—and you feel, somehow, that you alone are the inauthentic one.

Far from spoiled, the young people who have written to me don't seem to feel like they deserve happiness. They feel self-conscious and guilty about everything they do. They can't move forward without feeling like they're stepping on someone's toes. They often resolve to seem better, to work harder, to keep their mouths shut at the exact moments when they need to speak up and tell the truth in order to feel right with the world. They feel afraid of showing their true selves because they're sure they'll be shamed for it. Everyone is waiting to be exposed as a fake. As far as I can tell, twentysomethings don't embody the self-assured, self-promotional values of social media any more than Gen-Xers like me do; it's just that they've learned that one should never publicly reveal one's doubts, anxieties, and ambivalence. I have spent years peeking behind the stage curtain, and I can see how excruciatingly difficult it is for them to hold that pose.

I started writing advice at the early webzine *Suck.com* in May 2001. I had been writing cartoons for the site for years; the advice was just an experiment. But I continued to answer advice letters on my blog when *Suck* went under a month later. Back then, advice columns were more prescriptive, pedantic, problem-focused. I was less interested in such concrete hazards than I was in the broader poisons of our culture, how we ingest and metabolize them until they feel like a part of us, yet we still can't figure out why we're sick. "Avoiding confrontation is bad for you," I wrote in one early blog post. "Dishonesty in one of your relationships tends to leak into all the others." I was thirty-one years old, unemployed, a little depressed, and avoiding confrontation with the older divorced guy I was dating. I wanted to be honest, but I also wanted to be loved. These things were already starting to seem like they might be at odds with each other.

But there was still some breathing room for messiness back then, at least online. These days, it's not hard to notice how careful image management and aggressive self-promotion and anxieties about "staying on brand" have seeped into the online mix. We've integrated all the pressures of the commercial realm into our personal lives, applying the same competitive expectations to love, friendship, family, and even our internal state of mind. Teenagers and twentysomethings have grown up with social media, which means they have been doing this their whole lives. And the pressure that creates is enormous: Not only do many of us now expect to make money at creative careers that used to be seen as the poverty-stricken purview of a small handful of artists, but we also expect to establish a name for ourselves quickly, to find our work deeply satisfying, and to become famous overnight—or at least to have tens of thousands of followers. This pervasive, subconscious longing is the background noise generated by the new digital realm, like the terrible hiss and hum of an old refrigerator. And it affects all of us, even if the pain it causes is most visible in the young. It tells us that no matter what our circumstances might be, we should be dressing like fashion bloggers and vacationing like celebrities and eating like food critics and fucking like porn stars, and if we aren't, we're losers who are doomed to non-greatness forever and ever.

Most people don't consciously believe any of these things, of course—teenagers or fifty-year-olds. We may believe that we just want to muddle through the day without screwing up or embarrassing ourselves. But screwing up and embarrassing ourselves turn out to be the meat of what many of us experience these days, because behind the hazy filter of our conscious desires lie those obscenely inflated expectations. And merely muddling through, doing your best, seeing friends when you can, trying to enjoy yourself as much as possible is, according to the reigning dictates of today's culture, tantamount to failure. You must live your best life and be the best version of yourself; otherwise you're nothing and no one.

It gets worse. We now recognize that getting the lives we want depends on cultivating the right attitude, so we beat ourselves up every time our state of mind is less than 100 percent optimistic. If there's a mass religion of global culture, it's the high-capitalist belief, trumpeted at every turn by every single voice in the spotlight, that by believing in yourself without fail, you can get everything you've ever dreamed of. It all depends on your faith, your ability to squelch the doubts in your head that arise when yet another glamorous on-brand winner pops up in your Instagram feed.

Very few people tell you anymore that those doubts in your head are part of the noise you hear when you're alive, full stop. Very few people explain that success rarely happens quickly, and that even if it does, there are still lingering worries and bad days and hours and hours of tedious work involved. There aren't many inspirational quotes about how discouragement will plague you as you work and that's just how it feels to work at something difficult. There aren't many memes reminding you that you won't get everything you dream of— and that getting everything you dream of might not make you happy anyway, no matter what that constantly scrolling feed of highly curated "best lives" seems to imply.

Obviously, as an advice columnist, I'm often at risk of becoming part of the problem. I tell people to believe in the lives they really want, to set their expectations high and strive tirelessly to achieve their dreams. But I also want to say to them, time after time, that there is no "better version" of you waiting in the future. The best version of you is who you are right here, right now, in this fucked-up, impatient, imperfect, sublime moment. Shut out the noise and enjoy exactly who you are and what you have, right here, right now.

tag and release

Today I have to go to the Department of Motor Vehicles to get my driver's license renewed. My current license photo is ten years old, so old that the carefree woman in the picture always takes me by surprise. Her hair looks unnaturally shiny. Her smile says, "I have nowhere in particular to be. Let's go grab a cocktail!" Today I have to say goodbye to that lighthearted girl, and welcome her older, more harried replacement. Today I have to stand in poorly marked lines with impatient strangers, reading signs about what we can and cannot do, what we should and should not expect.

Last time I got my license renewed, the first picture was so bad that the DMV guy laughed out loud. I was young and carefree then, so it didn't bother me. "Show me," I commanded. He turned the screen around. My eyes were half-closed and my mouth was screwed up in a weird knot. Remember that scene in the movie *Election* where they pause the image just as Tracy Flick, the wannabe school president played by Reese Witherspoon, looks drunk and deranged? It was like that. The next photo turned out great, though, because I couldn't stop smiling about the first one.

That's not the mood I'm in today. Today, if the same thing happens, I'll grumble. They'll take a second crappy photo of me and no one will be laughing. To them, I'll be just another angry lady to tag and release back onto the wild freeways of Los Angeles. When you visit the DMV, you realize that you can bestride the narrow world like a colossus for only so long—namely, until you're about thirty-nine. After that, you're not special anymore. You're just another indistinct face in a sea of the nobodies.

I have all of my father's old driver's licenses. That's the kind of thing you save when somebody dies—not their unpublished papers, not their shelves full of books. You save the evidence of their trips to the DMV. Something about those little snapshots of my dad's face, four years older, and then four years older again, standing up against that dark-red background they once used in North Carolina, slows my pulse a little and makes me find the nearest chair. My father was not one to smile for these photos. He did, however, open his eyes a little wider as the years went by, possibly to make himself look less old and grouchy.

On March 5, 1973, he wore a red gingham shirt and matching red tie. He was about to turn thirty-four. On March 10, 1981, he wore a V-neck sweater over a maroon shirt. He was about to turn forty-two, and he looked fitter than he was at age thirty-four. On March 14, 1985, my father looked as tan as George Hamilton. On March 13, 1989, he was about to turn fifty, and he took his glasses off before they took the picture, maybe so he would look younger. His face was more calm and open than it was in the other shots. In his last license photo, taken on March 15, 1993, he had let his hair go gray, and he looked relaxed and happy. Two and a half years later, he went to bed feeling a little bit sick and died in his sleep of his first heart attack.

The fact of someone's premature death shouldn't make everything they ever did seem tragic, but sometimes it does anyway. I wish I had a slightly more uplifting story at the ready whenever I shuffled through these laminated cards. I wish I didn't feel quite so melancholy about his life, neatly sliced into four-year intervals, his face transforming from young to older to oldest. What was he feeling at each moment when the camera flashed in his face? What buried shame or sadness bubbled up, what bit of longing worked its way to the surface in the bleak light of that DMV office?

My father talked a lot about not wanting to get old. He visited his parents regularly, but it often depressed him. He didn't want to live the way they did, growing stooped and wrinkled, smoking and bickering as they circled the drain. Maybe he had an unusually strong fear of aging and death. He was very fit, and he was always juggling several girlfriends at once, most of them under thirty-five. Aging made him anxious.

Twenty-odd years later, I realize that *most* people are anxious about growing older, so much so that they're hesitant to say it out loud. We can't quite believe that we're mortal and we'll age just like everybody else. At a certain point, we start counting the years we might have left, if we're lucky. We become more pragmatic. We take what we can get. We don't need big signs to tell us what we should and should not expect.

—

Ten years ago, when that last driver's license photo was taken, I was thirty-three years old and I weighed 125 pounds. In the photo, my face is lean and tan because I went hiking every single morning. I worked from home and made good money as a freelance writer. I read a lot. I adopted houseplants. I wrote songs on my guitar. I was so young. I had no idea how young I was.

But before you go flipping between the thirty-three-year-old, with her broad smile, and the forty-three-year-old, with her vague look of world-weariness, keep in mind all the things that happened in the ten years in between: I dumped my boyfriend. I found a full-time job. I bought a house. I got married. My stepson moved in. I had a daughter. I wrote a book. I had another daughter. I quit my job. A close friend died of cancer.

When you glance from one license to the next, you don't see the long nights I spent tossing and turning, working up the courage to ditch my boyfriend. You don't see me painting the walls of my house alone, trying to accept my uncertain future. You can't see me driving through the south of Spain with my future husband, or see me big and pregnant a year later, pulling weeds out of our front yard in a fit of hormonal mania. You don't see me crying in the car after I left the baby at day care for the first time. You don't see me at the beach with my kids, smearing sunscreen on my face and hoping that no one eats sand when I'm not looking. You don't see my hands shaking as I crush up pills, trying to help my friend die a peaceful death, wondering if there even is such a thing.

A lot can happen in ten years. You can't be carefree forever. But when I was just thirty-three, I thought that I would never have the bad taste to grow old, let alone allow it to depress me. I thought I was better than this. What is youth, but the ability to nurse a superiority complex beyond all reason, to suspend disbelief indefinitely, to imagine yourself immune to the plagues and perils faced by other mortal humans? But one day, you wake up and you realize that you're not immune.

When my driver's license photo arrives a week later, it feels like an omen of my impending decline. My hair is limp and scraggly. I have dark circles under my eyes. I look like the "after" photo in one of those photo-essays on the ravages of crystal meth. I have the blank but guilty look of a sex offender.

It's maybe the shittiest photo of me ever taken, and now I have to carry it with me everywhere I go. On the bright side, my husband and I spend a good half hour passing the license back and forth, laughing at how hideous it is. But privately, I wonder if I have the face of a woman who missed out on something. This is the shape my mid-life crisis is taking: I'm worried about what I have time to accomplish before I get too old to do anything. I'm fixated on what my life should look like by now. I'm angry at myself, because I should look better, I should be in better shape, I should be writing more, I should be a better cook and a more present, enthusiastic mother.

—

Sometimes I go online looking for inspiration, but all I find is evidence that everyone in the world is more energetic than me. Thanks to blogs and Twitter and Facebook, I can sift through the proof that hundreds of other people aren't slouching through life. They're thriving in their big houses in beautiful cities, they're cooking delicious organic meals for their children, they're writing timely thank-you notes to their aunts and uncles and mothers for the delightful gift that was sent in the mail and arrived right on time for Nina's third birthday.

Facebook makes me forget those weary strangers at the DMV. Suddenly it feels like the whole world is populated by highly effective, hip professional women, running around

from yoga classes to writing workshops, their fashionable out-
fits pulled taut over their abs of steel, chirping happily at each
other about the upcoming publication of their second poetry
chapbook—which is really going to make the move to the
remodeled loft a little hectic, but hey, that's life when you're
beautifulish and smartish and hopelessly productive!

It's not enough that I know all about their countless hobbies
and activities and pet projects and book clubs. I'm also treated
to professional-looking shots of their photogenic families,
their handsome, successful husbands and their darling children who are always hugging kittens or laughing joyfully on
pristine beaches, children who are filled with wonder around
the clock. Their children never pee in their Tinker Bell undies
by accident and then whine about going commando, just for
example. But maybe that's because their children have parents
who never lose their tempers or heat up frozen fish sticks for
dinner or forget to do the laundry. Their kids have parents
who let them sleep under the stars at Joshua Tree, and no one
soils her sleeping bag or has a bad trip from too many corn-
syrup-infused juice boxes.

Dear sweet merciful lord, deliver me from these deliri-
ously happy parents, frolicking in paradise, publishing books,
competing in triathlons, crafting jewelry, speaking to at-risk
youth, painting birdhouses, and raving about the new cardio
ballet place that gives you an ass like a basketball. Keep me
safe from these serene, positive-thinking hipster moms, with
their fucking handmade recycled crafts and their mid-century-
modern furniture and their glowing skin and their optimism
and their happy-go-lucky posts about their family's next trip
to a delightful boutique hotel in Bali.

I am physically incapable of being that effective or that effusive. I can't knit and do yoga and smile at strangers *and* apply
mascara every morning. These people remind me that I'll never

magically become the kind of person who shows up on time, looks fabulous, launches a multimillion-dollar business, and travels the world.

When I was younger, I thought I might wake up one day and be different: more sophisticated, more ambitious, more organized. Back then, my ambivalence and my odd shoes and my bad hair seemed more like a statement. When you're young, being sloppy and cynical and spaced-out looks good on you. But my flaws don't feel so excusable anymore. "I need to fix everything," a voice inside keeps telling me. It's time to be an efficient professional human, at long last, and a great mother and an adoring wife. It's time to shower regularly while I'm at it.

No matter how hard I try to will myself into some productive adult's reality, though, I'm still that forty-three-year-old superfreak in my driver's license photo. Someday, one of my daughters will hold this license in her hand and feel sorry for me, long after I'm gone. "She was only forty-three in this one. But, Jesus, look at that awful hair. And that expression on her face. Why does she look so upset? Or is that fear? What was she so afraid of?" I don't want my daughters to look at me—then or now—and see someone who's disappointed in herself. At the very least, I have to change that.

—

Early one Sunday morning, when I was running out to get some groceries, I saw a woman standing on the sidewalk, waving a Yard Sale sign around. She was smiling as she shook this big piece of cardboard with something scrawled on it. You could barely read the words. The writing was in ballpoint pen, and maybe she ran out of room for the address because the last part was squeezed in below, and there was a huge space under the words anyway. But she seemed pleased with her sign. This confused me, because if I had made a sign like that myself, I would've ripped it up, declaring it unacceptable. After that, I probably would've complained about how I didn't have any more goddamn poster board to start another sign, and I probably would've blamed my husband for not buying more poster board at the drugstore. "When I say get *some* poster board, that word 'some' means *more than one piece.*"

I would've panicked and started a fight, over something as small as a Yard Sale sign. But I also wouldn't have agreed to stand on the curb with my bad sign, drawing attention to myself. No way. If I were her, I would've made my husband stand on the corner with the sign. And I still would've blamed him when the yard sale got too crowded and hectic. "Where have you been? I can't handle this whole thing on my own! This was YOUR IDEA IN THE FIRST PLACE!"

That morning, I sat at the intersection in my idling car and watched the woman jumping around, looking thrilled about her newly improvised role as street barker, and even though I was in a bad mood, she made me smile. She had swagger. She didn't care that her sign sucked. And the drivers in the cars next to me were smiling, too. Her raw joy was infectious. We all gave her appreciative, you-made-my-morning waves. *We liked the cut of her jib.*

I used to be more like that woman, having fun with whatever task was in front of me instead of freaking out about how I looked to other people. I need to figure out how to get back there. My life has turned out great. So why am I comparing myself to some perfectly styled, enviable, energetic professional in my head? It's like I keep ripping up the stupid sign and starting over. I keep saying to myself: "This is all wrong. *You* are all wrong." I keep saying: "You should be a shiny, infallible adult by now. Why are you still such a mess?"

I want to be more like that woman on the curb—or the way I imagine that she must be, based on my brief sighting of her, jumping around on that gray sidewalk in the dim light of the early morning. She isn't afraid of falling short. No one can tell her what she can and can't do, what she should and should not expect. She's not losing sleep over the mid-century-modern furniture she doesn't own, or the organic dairy farms in Wisconsin she hasn't visited. Maybe her house needs to be vacuumed, or maybe it's spotless. Maybe she dresses fashionably and does her makeup perfectly every morning, or maybe her hair color always needs a touch-up. It doesn't matter either way, because she doesn't view these things as verdicts on her character. She knows how to savor what she has. She doesn't ask herself whether or not she has it all. She has more important things to do.

haunted

aunted houses are designed to make their guests feel small and powerless, but also a tiny bit titillated in spite of themselves. Suspense builds slowly. Each creepy revelation incites curiosity first, then dread, then horror. The point is to seduce these unsuspecting mortals into exploring their darkest corners, only to reduce them to a quivering pile of nerves. The best haunted houses don't murder their guests. Instead, they slowly and sublimely drive them mad.

For headstrong women who know their own desires, growing up in conventional society sometimes feels like inhabiting a haunted house. At first, there is so much promise, mysterious and tantalizing. As you pull open that heavy wooden door with the gargoyle knocker, you feel flattered by its intimidating proportions—you are necessary and important, maybe for the first time ever. But soon you catch fleeting glimpses of dark spirits who whisper in douche-bro baritones that you don't belong and never will. You develop a recurring suspicion that you're merely a pawn in some elaborate game, that even if you're brave you can never be a real player. The floor shifts under your feet, the walls shake, you awake at midnight to heavy breathing. "She was asking for it" is scrawled across the wall in blood. You tell your story the next morning, but no one believes you. Did you imagine the whole thing? Is some unearthly force trying to make you feel weak and lost? Or are you just losing your mind?

This kind of suspenseful badgering, with its malevolent and condescending patriarchal undertones, pervades Shirley Jackson's work. In the novels and many of the stories she wrote in the middle of the twentieth century, the polite banter of seemingly innocent common folk develops into outright mockery, subterfuge, or even violence. When confronted by an unexpectedly hostile world, Jackson's female protagonists experience a climactic rush of bafflement and betrayal that inevitably spills over into a more private realm of second-guessing, self-doubt, and paranoia.

Jackson relished untangling the process by which women lose themselves. She could stretch the ordeal out over the course of an entire novel, as she did in *The Haunting of Hill House* (1959), with the slow unraveling of lonely thirty-two-year-old Eleanor Vance. Or she could foreshadow the whole harrowing experience in forty-odd pages, as she did with the start of her novel *Hangsaman* (1951), which reads like a modern parable of disempowerment.

Jackson took ordinary settings—a mundane California suburb, an ordinary small town—and transformed them into eerie and frightening places where regular people were unable to overcome their worst impulses or push back against the malevolent initiatives of the mob. In Jackson's vision, even smart bystanders could be at once suspicious of and vulnerable to the delusions, false gods, and blunt weapons of the rabble. Reading her work today sometimes feels like discovering a detailed prophecy not just of rape culture but of the vitriolic thugs who seem to rule the internet and have somehow invaded our politics. Seven decades before Donald Trump's outraged mobs in MAGA hats, Jackson unveiled the brutality and contempt that lurk beneath the surface of neighborly human interactions. From "The Lottery," her seminal portrait of a murderous horde of ordinary folks published in *The New Yorker* in 1948, to her final chilling novel, *We Have Always Lived in the Castle* (1962), in which a hostile gaggle of villagers harasses two sisters isolated in their dead parents' lonely house, Jackson felt compelled to sound the alarm on humanity: Individuals might have unseen talents and untold potential, but groups, under the sway of pernicious traditions and narcissistic leaders, inevitably become unruly, self-serving, and hostile.

Jackson came to such stories honestly. According to Ruth Franklin's biography, *Shirley Jackson: A Rather Haunted Life,* Jackson's mother hectored her mercilessly about her weight and bad habits from the time she was a child until the last days of her life. (Jackson died of an apparent heart attack in 1965, at the age of forty-eight.) The importance of keeping up appearances in polite society was central to Jackson's affluent upbringing in Burlingame, California, and Rochester, New York. Her mother's family was firmly grounded among San Francisco's wealthy elite, and her father was an executive in the printing business. But appearances were something Jackson rejected from an early age with her unruly auburn hair, unconventional style of dress, caustic wit, and swagger. And even though Jackson was confident and outspoken, she could find intimacy dangerous, a dark realm of judgment and scrutiny and deeply personal insults that—not surprising, given her mother's fixation on social standing—seemed to carry the verdict of the wider culture.

By the time Jackson, then twenty-one, met her husband, the *New Yorker* writer and literary critic Stanley Edgar Hyman, she was primed to accept condescension, belittling, and neglect as her natural habitat, according to Franklin. Early letters show that Hyman loved Jackson dearly and admired her work enormously—maybe that wasn't so easy, considering that his own writing career, though impressive, stalled just as Jackson's was taking off. For her part, Jackson was sure at the start of their relationship that she could control Hyman, and he didn't dispute that claim. "I am proud, and completely powerful," Jackson wrote of one of their first nights together.

But Hyman soon proved an emotionally inconstant mate, alternating between adoration and disdain. He regularly cheated on Jackson, then relayed the details of his dalliances in letters to her. There was the "Polish slut of twenty-six" who was "damned good-looking in a consumptive way"; the three bohemian girls he met at a party ("I fondled them all indiscriminately [and] called all three of them 'baby'"); and the cute redhead in the apartment upstairs he romanced while Jackson was on vacation with her family.

Like any critic worth his salt, Hyman found ready justification for his behavior in ideology. In his view, enlightened bohemians recognized that monogamy was a faulty construct designed for high-capitalist sheep. Jackson wrote him angry letters about his affairs, but rarely sent them. "You mustn't be so timid with Stanley," a mutual friend told her. "You let him categorize you and your emotions and your reactions just like he does his own." Instead, Jackson endured Hyman's treatment of her, as Franklin writes, choosing to "swallow her rage at his infidelity."

No slouch herself at compartmentalizing, Jackson managed to raise four children, mostly in a somewhat insular town in Vermont, the home of Bennington College, where Hyman taught literature. (Jackson once wrote of the faculty wife, "She is always just the teensiest bit in the way.") By all reports, Jackson charted her own course through the domestic expectations placed on her. A great cook, she balked at cleaning or playing the traditional, self-sacrificing mother but spent lots of time singing and reading books to her children. And while Jackson relished the magic of two smart women bonding (a staple of her work), she didn't seem to have that many close, lasting female friendships in real life—though not for lack of effort on her part. Even the pairs of women and girls in Jackson's novels are inevitably threatened by jealousy, betrayal, and the larger forces (manipulative paramours, bloodthirsty mobs, supernatural beings) working against them. As Franklin keenly observes, "One of the ironies of Jackson's fiction is the essential role that women play in enforcing the standards of the community—standards that hurt them most."

In a biography densely packed with anecdotes, letters, highly detailed descriptions, and lengthy, thoughtful analyses of most of Jackson's work, Franklin paints a picture of Jackson as creatively fulfilled but isolated and unhappy. She relied on Hyman for critical feedback, but resented her dependence on him. She struggled with anxiety, struggled with her weight, struggled with nightmares and sleepwalking. Like many women of her generation, she was prescribed tranquilizers for her problems. Even as her work life began to thrive, and she eventually became the primary breadwinner—thanks in large part to her best-selling essay collection on domestic foibles, *Life Among the Savages*—Jackson felt alienated and emotionally starved. She had difficulty trusting people. And with her husband pursuing an ongoing affair with her close friend, who could blame her?

No wonder so many of Jackson's works conjure a slow, simmering resentment that becomes almost hallucinatory, as if years of muting emotional reactions naturally warp perception, fueling a state of delirium. Franklin highlights this dynamic throughout her biography, tracing the lineage of belittlement from Jackson's mother to her husband, and underscoring the ways that Jackson was "shamed . . . for legitimate and rational desires." Indeed, Jackson often wrote in journals and letters that she felt tricked by Hyman: "You once wrote me a letter . . . telling me that I would never be lonely again. I think that was the first, the most dreadful, lie you ever told me." It is grimly fitting that when one of her purest dramatizations of this feeling of being misunderstood and manipulated, *The Bird's Nest* (1954), was adapted as a film (*Lizzie*), the heroine wasn't depicted as "hysterical," the victim of emotional strains, both familial and social. She was portrayed as a flat-out lunatic.

But for Jackson, the heroine's destruction always begins with false promises—from parents, from lovers, from society at large. The process is embodied perhaps most brilliantly at the start of *Hangsaman*. At her parents' garden party, the seventeen-year-old ingenue Natalie Waite meets a strikingly confident woman named Verna, who tells her, "Little Natalie, never rest until you have uncovered your essential self. Remember that. Somewhere, deep inside you, hidden by all sorts of fears and worries and petty little thoughts, is a clean pure being made of radiant colors."

Later, though, Natalie's mother drunkenly rages over her husband's betrayals in a bedroom upstairs. "First they tell you lies," she says to Natalie, "and they make you believe them. Then they give you a little of what they promised, just a little, enough to keep you thinking you've got your hands on it. Then you find out that you're tricked, just like everyone else, just like *everyone*, and instead of being different and powerful and giving the orders, you've been tricked just like everyone else and then you begin to know what happens to everyone and how they all get tricked."

A now-tipsy Natalie escapes downstairs, but a strange older man presses her to tell him what she's thinking. "About how wonderful I am," she replies. The man seems angered by this, and leads her into the woods. Natalie's innocent shock at his intentions is truly heart-stopping: "'Oh my dear God sweet Christ,' Natalie thought, so sickened she nearly said it aloud, 'is he going to *touch* me?'"

Jackson understood horror. She knew that horror requires an emotional seduction, one that is revealed to be a malevolent ruse: The ingenue experiences herself as radiant and powerful right before her power is stripped from her. Clever young girls imagine they were born to be cherished, when instead they're created merely to be destroyed. In many of her stories, Jackson outlines how girls are groomed for this fate by overly critical mothers (or, in the case of *Hangsaman,* by a manipulatively intimate father). Worst of all, the recognition that the macabre universe you enter in maturity isn't fantasy—it's reality—sets you apart in the world, raving or drunk in some upstairs bedroom. Your choice is either to play along, or to lose your grip completely.

Whether that sounds hopelessly bleak to the point of paranoia or terrifyingly prescient depends on your particular perch. For me, Jackson's uncanny portraits of the fragmentation and collapse of the female psyche echo throughout contemporary culture, from the casual derision we lavish on all things female or feminine to the so-called fairy-tale marriages we celebrate in the pages of magazines, the ones that are later revealed to be nightmares of verbal and physical abuse. The chilling seven-thousand-word letter a sexual-assault victim wrote to her Stanford attacker in 2016 (which quickly went viral) reads like a Jackson novel in miniature, in which darkness subsumes former innocence. By its end, we hear echoes of the last, haunting line of "The Lottery": "And then they were upon her." But has the world gone mad, or have we?

These feelings of dread and panic, paired with the desperate hope that the deluded crowd will snap out of it and come to its senses, lie at the heart of what makes Shirley Jackson's work unforgettable. Tapping into her own frustrations and agonies, she painted one exquisite portrait after another of that precise juncture where blustery confidence yields to helplessness and terror. The sinister forces the heroine perceives are real, but they're just ephemeral enough, by design, to make her doubt herself repeatedly. In the end, the self-possessed woman becomes the possessed.

———

In order to understand how women land at the point where their desires are treated as utterly beside the point, it's important to zoom in on that moment when the ingénue first enters the haunted house. That moment forces us to recall the naïve bluster of girlhood with an almost bittersweet clarity, and remember, in a rush, how all of the stories we were told at a young age seemed to place us at the center of everything: The witch was waiting for us, sure, but we would win in the end. Beauty and innocence always win—or that's what girls are usually told, up to the exact moment when most of what they've been taught to value proves worthless.

And yet: To be a girl again! Not a child, of course, but an inhabitant of that rarefied, pH-balanced zone of romance and optimism, where you might flirt and flounce and be easily bruised by a pea. Girls can put on a dress and twirl in a circle and others will clap and say, "How pretty!" Girls never have to question whether the attention they get is well-meaning. They skip through the forest with a basket full of treats for Grandma, happily telling every Big Bad Wolf they encounter exactly where they're headed.

Sooner or later, of course, most of us wise up. A combination of skepticism and feminist indignation sets in, and it becomes harder to wink coyly at strangers or to marvel innocently at Grandma's sharp and pointy teeth.

But for those of us who retain some sense memory of twirling and hearing others coo, spotting the word "girl" in every other title these days (*Girls, Gone Girl, 2 Broke Girls, The Girl on the Train, The Girl Before, New Girl, The Girl with the Dragon Tattoo,* to name just a few) can bring on a faintly nostalgic twinge. Or is it a shudder? We recall that privileged but exasperating era when we were transfixing and special but also a little doomed. As a girl, you are a delicate glass vase, waiting to be broken. You are a sweet-smelling flower, waiting for life's hobnailed boots to trample you. That built-in suspense is part of your appeal.

"How will you make it on your own?" the theme song of *The Mary Tyler Moore Show* asks, hinting that the slightest pothole in the road might ruin everything for our hopeful heroine, peering worriedly from behind her steering wheel. When books and movies and TV shows use the word "girl" in their titles, it's this state of uncertainty they're hoping to conjure. Forget that Mary Richards herself was done with twirling, if not hat tossing, well before she stepped into Mr. Grant's newsroom. Ever since she (and "That Girl" Marlo Thomas before her) turned the world on with her smile, we've been offered coquettish creatures who mimic her second-guessing and nervous tics but often lack her complexity and gravitas.

With their forced laughs and their preening and those heavy bangs resting straight on their eyeballs, many among the current batch of TV ingénues seem designed to conjure the childlike poutiness of America's onetime sweetheart Ally McBeal. You can afford to be a little sassy and street smart when you have big doll eyes and the frame of a preteen. With a few exceptions—Tina Fey's Liz Lemon on *30 Rock,* Amy Poehler's Leslie Knope on *Parks and Recreation,* the title character on *Fleabag*—we were largely spared confident, complicated, single comedic heroines for a few decades straight. Each week on *2 Broke Girls,* the spunky leads fled confrontation, sought solace in each other's "You go, girl!" clichés, and then strode out from their hidey-holes to shake a finger in someone's face, only to be rewarded with more humiliation. For all of the single-girl bluster of *Whitney,* our heroine had few interests outside of her live-in boyfriend, whether turning him on, manipulating him, or distracting him from ogling another girl's assets. Even Jess (Zooey Deschanel) of *New Girl,* the least insipid of the lot, tended to go all bashful and pigeon-toed a few times per episode, forsaking weightier goals in favor of trotting out her oddball charms for the adoration of her male roommates.

After prolonged exposure to these smoldering doll-babies, it was hard not to long for some of the stubbornness of Lucy Ricardo (Lucille Ball), the insatiability and bad temper of Samantha Jones (Kim Cattrall), or the nerve and self-possession of Mary Richards. When Mary and Rhoda attended a party thrown by young hippies and Mary noticed that they were the only ones wearing eyeliner, we understood Mary and Rhoda as real human beings, complex entities capable of layered reactions to their surroundings. If this were *2 Broke Girls,* Mary and Rhoda would have dashed off to the bathroom to giggle behind their hands, then wiped off their makeup and reemerged, anxious to blend in with the crowd. Or Rhoda, after resolving to tell those hippie kids a thing or two, would've ended up being humiliated by them in the process.

For decades, in books and movies and on TV, humiliation has been used to transform adult women into something lighter, perkier, less frightening. It's as if writers imagine that we're afraid of proud women and we're eager to see them humbled. Female characters are outfitted with charming tics ("What an adorable sneeze!") and inoffensive mediocrities ("She's so clumsy!") and toothless yuppie righteousness ("You tell that snippy barista the customer is always right!"). Such narratives favor the naïve audacity of girlhood over more robust concepts of femininity; the grit and complexity of Deborah Harry or Kim Gordon or Björk are inevitably upstaged by the lip-glossy pep and nonthreatening lady bluster of Katy Perry or Taylor Swift. (Beyoncé, with her brazen bird-flipping and baseball-bat-swinging, is the exception that proves the rule.) Even shows like *Big Little Lies* and *Crazy Ex-Girlfriend* induce a certain familiar queasiness, as their grown female characters still occasionally twirl for an imagined audience. It's enough to make you long for the frank assertiveness of Mary or Rhoda or even Carrie Bradshaw, who, in all of her attention-seeking wishy-washiness, at least had the courage of conviction to dress like an extra in the Ziegfeld Follies.

—

When Lena Dunham's HBO comedy, *Girls,* premiered in 2012, Dunham looked poised to skip through the woods for a while, then toss the basket of cupcakes aside and play the Big Bad Wolf instead. It was no accident that we met our lead, Hannah (played by Dunham), while she was slurping up pasta on her parents' dime, and that, just a few scenes later, she was having awkward sex on the couch with Adam (Adam Driver), a guy who rarely returned her texts. The deliberately jarring juxtaposition of these images, one of an overgrown infant, the other of a sexually submissive woman, was at once horrifying and hilariously appropriate. Caught in that bewildering nowhereland between childhood and adulthood, Hannah demonstrated how easy it could be to experience a loss of directional cues, if not a total shutdown of onboard instrument panels. The show's use of that ubiquitous term "girl" was less about offering up another candidate for America's sweetheart than it was about charting that unnerving intersection of giggly specialness and self-consciousness, coyness and skepticism, flirtation and feminist indignation.

Hannah herself appeared to have marched straight from a Take Back the Night rally to a booty call with a guy who wanted her to pretend she was a lost girl on the street with a Cabbage Patch Kids lunchbox. She played along, limply— "Yeah, I was really scared." But a few minutes later, when Adam called her friend's abortion a "heavy situation," she asserted that it was less a tragic affair than a pragmatic concern. "What was she gonna do, like, have a baby and then take it to her babysitting job? It's not realistic."

If *Girls* was at first heralded as game-changing television, there was a reason for that: The stuttered confessions, half-smiles, hissed warnings, and quiet shared confidences between Hannah and her friends made the empty sassing and high-fiving of existing girlie comedies look like the spasms of a bygone era. But what was most riveting about Hannah and her friends was not their wisdom, righteousness, or backbone—as we might imagine would be the antidote to the frothy pap of other female-dominated comedies—but their confusion, their vulnerability, and their ambivalence. Instead of clamoring for attention like Whitney or Jess, Hannah's roommate, Marnie (Allison Williams), who was beautiful and had a devoted boyfriend, was bored by his sensitivity, bored by his affection (she complained that "his touch now feels like a weird uncle putting his hand on my knee at Thanksgiving"), but couldn't muster the resolve to dump him. This was not how the candy-coated ingénue of America's imagining, poised on the doorstep of womanhood, was supposed to react to male attention.

Hannah, meanwhile, almost never took a stand in the show's first two seasons. She asked her boss at her publishing internship to give her a paid job, and he politely bid her farewell in that passive-aggressive professional way that's so difficult to counter. After trading quips with a potential employer at an interview, Hannah said something off-color and was summarily dismissed for her insensitivity. (She was baffled but didn't protest.) Worst of all, she let her sort-of-not-really-boyfriend, Adam, call her a dirty little whore and smash her face into the mattress. Afterward, he asked her if she wanted a Gatorade. "What flavor?" she asked. "Orange," he answered. "Um, no thanks, I'm good," she replied. This was how far she was willing to go to express a preference: a polite no thanks, maybe next time.

In the show's early seasons, Hannah, like so many women walking the line between the coddling of girlhood and the realities of adulthood, didn't hoot or cackle or tell it like it is the way other sassy female leads on TV did. Her inability to do that, against a backdrop of smart-talking but empty comedic heroines, felt like a groundbreaking choice. Because most young women, even the assertive and determined ones, still find themselves, in those forlorn in-between years, apologizing repeatedly, blurting some muddled, half-finished thought and, finally, resolving to take up less space.

It's telling that, as Hannah aged and stood up for herself more, audiences and critics seemed less enamored of her antics. Part of this was a natural backlash to Dunham's massive fame. After the first few seasons aired, Dunham had become a kind of cultural icon, with a newsletter, a memoir, and a million and one outspoken remarks to share. As her confidence (and wealth and notoriety) grew, her tone shifted from the naïve enthusiasm of a young woman to the self-assured bafflement of a grown woman who's maybe just a little bit tired of twirling in circles. But by then, the audience had started to roll its eyes: America's sweetheart always gets too big for her britches eventually.

The discord between how vehemently we're told to believe in ourselves as young girls and how dismissively we're treated as young women when we dare to do so—captured so heartbreakingly over the course of six seasons of *Girls*—is part of what fuels the shudder brought on by that word, "girl." As vivid as our culture's fantasy of this magical juncture between childhood and adulthood might be, it's hardly a carefree time occupied by effusive pixies, let alone a period to which most of us would happily return. Because one day, we wake up ready—not to wag our fingers in someone's face (which is just another way of twirling when you get right down to it) but to present our true selves without apology. This is the trajectory that Lena Dunham and her collaborators ended up portraying, with humor and subtlety and realism at first, and then through a haze of self-consciousness, self-righteous rage, and resignation as the show drew to a close. After all, you can only turn the world on with your smile for so long before it gets a little dull.

Eventually, we have to learn to assert what we will and won't accept. That might be less funny and less cute, but *that* is how you make it on your own, as Mary Richards often demonstrated, though her voice sometimes trembled and her hands sometimes shook. That's the reason that scene where Mary throws her hat in the air still feels exhilarating, nearly fifty years later. Something in that arc of her hat in the air, something in that expectant smile, told us that she was a little too hopeful, a little too sure that everything would turn out swell (as she might put it). Because that's not how it usually goes. You think the world will cheer you on forever, but at some point, the cheers curdle into jeers. You can't twirl anymore. You want to believe in yourself, but you have your doubts. You don't always trust your instincts. But how can you? The adoring crowd has become an angry mob. You must be doing something wrong.

—

Even as smart, confident adult female characters have paraded onto the small screen over the past few years, the more astute and capable these women prove to be, the more likely it is that they're also completely nuts. And by "nuts" I don't mean complicated, difficult, thorny, or complex—the token "crazy" that women are so readily assigned. I mean that these characters are often portrayed as volcanoes that could blow at any minute. Or worse, the very abilities and skills that make them singular and interesting come coupled with hideous psychic deficiencies.

On *Veep*, Julia Louis-Dreyfus's character is ambitious and manipulative because she's selfish. On *Nurse Jackie*, Jackie was an excellent RN in part because she was self-medicated into a state of calm. On *The Killing*, Detective Linden, the world-weary, cold-souled cop, was a tenacious investigator in part because she was obsessive and damaged and a pretty negligent mother. And then there's *Homeland*, on which Carrie Mathison, the nearly clairvoyant CIA agent, is bipolar, unhinged, and recklessly promiscuous. These aren't just complicating characteristics like, say, Don Draper's infidelity or ambivalence. The suggestion on all of these shows is that a female character's flaws are inextricably linked to her strengths. Take away this pill problem or that personality disorder and the exceptional qualities vanish as well. And this is not always viewed as a tragedy: When Carrie undergoes electroconvulsive therapy to treat her bipolar disorder, we breathe a sigh of relief. Look how calm she is, enjoying a nice sandwich and sleeping peacefully in her childhood bed! But if she's happy, she's also forsaking her talents. And once she has a daughter and settles down, the implication is that while Carrie might be enjoying motherhood, her newfound peace is enjoyed at the world's expense.

The crazed antics of male characters like Don Draper, Walter White, or Dr. Gregory House are reliably treated as bold, fearless, even ultimately heroic (a daring remark saves the big account; a lunatic gesture scares off a murderous thug; an abrasive approach miraculously yields the answer that saves a young girl's life). In the case of Walter White in particular, he might've been making bad choices, but he was still the one doing the choosing. Female characters are rarely viewed as possessing such self-determination. Sure, there are notable exceptions, like the women of *Game of Thrones* and *Westworld*. But alongside every coolheaded Peggy Olson, we get hotheaded train-wreck characters who, like the ballerinas with lead weights around their ankles in Kurt Vonnegut's short story "Harrison Bergeron," can show no strength without an accompanying impediment to weigh them down.

Many of their flaws are fatal, or at least self-destructive, and they seem designed to invite censure. Time and again, we, the audience, are cast in the role of morally superior observers to these nut jobs. At times we might relate to a flash of anger, a fit of tears, a sudden urge to seduce a stranger in a bar; but we're constantly being warned that these behaviors aren't normal or admirable. They render these women out of step with the sane world.

Even as women have taken the lead on countless television shows over the past decade, they don't share the respect and dignity afforded their male counterparts. When Rebecca took an overdose on *Crazy Ex-Girlfriend*, or Nancy Botwin of *Weeds* endangered her kids by marrying a Mexican drug boss, or Carrie on *Homeland* chugged a tumbler of white wine then left the house to search for a one-night stand, we were meant to shake our heads at their bad choices. Their personality flaws or mental health issues were something they needed to be cured of or freed from—unlike, say, Monk, whose psychological tics were always portrayed as the adorable kernel of his genius.

Why should instability in men and women be treated so differently? "If you don't pull it together, no one will ever love you," a talking Barbie doll told Mindy during a fantasy on *The Mindy Project*, reminding us exactly what was always on the line for her. Don't act crazy, Mindy. Men don't like crazy.

"Women have often felt insane when cleaving to the truth of our experience," Adrienne Rich wrote. Women, with their tendency to "ask uncomfortable questions and make uncomfortable connections," as Rich puts it, are pathologized for the very traits that make them so formidable. Or, as Emily Dickinson wrote:

Much Madness is divinest Sense—
To a discerning Eye—
Much Sense—the starkest Madness—
'Tis the Majority

In this, as All, prevail—
Assent—and you are sane—
Demur—you're straightway dangerous—
And handled with a Chain—

—

"All smart women are crazy," I once told an ex-boyfriend in a heated moment, in an attempt to depict his future options as split down the middle between easygoing dimwits and sharp women who were basically just me with different hairstyles. By "crazy," I only meant "opinionated" and "moody" and "not always as pliant as one might hope." I was translating my personality into language he might understand—he who used "psycho-chick" as a stand-in for "noncompliant female" and whose idea of helpful counsel was "You're too smart for your own good," "my own good" presumably being a semi-vegetative state which precluded uncomfortable discussions about our relationship.

Over the years, "crazy" became my own reductive short-hand for every complicated, strong-willed woman I met. "Crazy" summed up the good and the bad in me and in all of my friends. Where I might have recognized that we were no crazier than anyone else in the world, instead I simply drew a larger and larger circle of crazy around us, lumping together anyone unafraid of confrontation, anyone who openly admit-ted her weaknesses, anyone who pursued agendas that might be out of step with the dominant cultural noise of the moment. "Crazy" became code for "interesting" and "courageous" and "worth knowing." I was trying to have a sense of humor about myself and those around me, trying to make room for stub-bornness and vulnerability and uncomfortable questions.

But I realize now, after watching these "crazy" characters

parade across my TV screen, that there's self-hatred in this act of self-subterfuge. "Our future depends on the sanity of each of us," Rich writes, "and we have a profound stake, beyond the personal, in the project of describing our reality as candidly and fully as we can to each other." Maybe this era of "crazy" women on TV was an unfortunate way station on the road from placid compliance to something more complex—something more like real life. Many so-called crazy women are smart women, that's all. They're not too smart for their own good, or for ours.

Ultimately, the challenges we face today are not unlike those Jackson faced as she began to speak publicly, embracing a wider community of writers in the years before her early death: to trust our senses, trust our instincts, trust that inside each of us is a "clean pure being made of radiant colors." Then we have to search the faces of the mob for signs of the same.

bravado

n the middle of the night, my husband's snores sometimes
sound like a cell phone vibrating. Other times, they sound
like waves crashing on a gravelly shore, or a minor chord
being played a little tentatively on a church organ, one low
note mixed with two wheezier, higher notes. Last night, they
sounded like the carriage return on a typewriter, the heavy,
industrial kind that's electric, but still gives a kick when the
carriage swings to the left side of the machine with a scratchy
clatter.

I loved to listen to that sound when I visited my mother's
office as a kid. Listening to her type 120 words a minute on an
IBM Selectric felt like an odd, percussive form of meditation. I
would lean way back in the swivel chair in her office and marvel at that sound of no-nonsense efficiency and capability in

action. She'd been a housewife since she married my dad, who was a professor. But after fifteen not-so-happy years together, she'd finally divorced him. Now she had three kids to feed, with no alimony and very little child support. Good thing she aced her typing class in high school.

Occasionally my mom would be interrupted by her boss, an older professor who wore tweedy English caps and argyle sweaters and pants that might best be described as jodhpurs. He would wander in with an unfocused look on his face and he'd ask where she'd put some papers he needed to send off. She'd stop and give him a strained smile that told me she'd taken care of these things days ago. The professor had giant shelves full of bound journal volumes in his office. Every few months, my mother would send away the flimsy-looking journals to the binder, and they'd return covered in leather, with gold lettering on the side. "Why does he do that?" I asked. "I don't know," she answered.

The professor didn't know how to type. He appeared not to know his own schedule, or even what day of the week it was. He could place a call, but sometimes he got confused if he had to put someone on hold and then take them off again. He would often stand in the doorway between his office and hers, his eyes watering slightly, his back a little stooped, and he'd hesitate to admit what bit of information he was struggling to retrieve. Even though he had all of the necessary levels of arrogance and condescension to have become a world-renowned neurobiologist with an endowed position, he didn't seem very capable of handling the mundane challenges of his life.

My mother would fight against this distracting presence for as long as she could stand, and then the suspense would be too great, and she'd interrupt her virtuoso typing solo, mid-measure.

A pause, maybe four quarter notes of silence. "Well?" she'd

say, a half note of whispery restraint, with an exasperated edge to it. My mother had been a straight-A math major in college. She was first chair clarinet in her high school band. She had all of the arrogance and condescension to have become a world-renowned neurobiologist, too. But she was a secretary instead, so she had a lot of shit to do.

———

Being capable isn't celebrated or embraced or rewarded handsomely or, often, even noticed these days. We prefer to celebrate the valiant, charismatic leader who speaks confidently of his vision of what should come next. We don't always care who is doing the concrete work to which his grand gestures allude. We don't demand that he demonstrate a clear understanding of the practical tasks and hurdles that lie in the path he's laid out. "Just make it happen" is what he tells anyone who asks, and that sounds bold and brave to us. Somehow, daring to insist that someone else do the work is admirable and just. Because he seems entitled to his visionary position, we are inclined to believe that he deserves it.

It's not surprising, I guess, that we coo and fawn over little boys who behave audaciously, while little girls armed with such arrogance often strike us as troublesome. And if a girl stubbornly holds fast to her strong sense of herself, the world is sure to chip away at it, day after day. "You sure think the world of yourself, young lady. Who do you think you are?"

For black girls and white girls and black boys and Asian girls and gay boys and anyone else not viewed as a so-called natural leader, confidence and swagger become leavened by self-doubt. We feel conflicted about speaking up or placing ourselves in the spotlight. When we talk, our statements can come out sounding slightly defensive, as if we're steeling ourselves against a blow: "I know you don't want to hear this, but I'm going to say it anyway."

But there's something else at work here, beyond direct rewards and punishments. There is also the pride of the capable, handed down as a kind of anticipatory salve for the marginalization to come. This is what my mom inculcated in me without necessarily knowing it. She had a different kind of arrogance than her boss did. Her arrogance said: *I'm* the one who handles everything here, and you, boss, are our bloviating, flaccid cover story. I am the journal article. You are the gold lettering on the side. I am the motor. You are the unreliable steering wheel. I am the gears of this machine. You are the pretty sparks that distract from the true industry.

I inherited this flavor of self-regard from her: the superior attitude of the supposedly inferior. Playing this role with pride, though, means sustaining contempt for the sounds that the bloviating, flaccid figurehead might make along the way to the conference, the gala, the speaking engagement. So I have spent most of my life rolling my eyes at the sound of bravado.

Bravado, if it made a noise, might sound like a major chord being played with great force on a chapel organ. That's the sound I think of when my husband is working on a talk "for the Chinese," or Skyping with one of his graduate students about how their work needs more work. My husband is not a blowhard, but he knows how to sound like one. He's not allergic to that sound. It's the sound of a throat being cleared for a little too long. It's the sound that a certain kind of facial expression makes, an expression that forms when encountering someone lower on the academic totem pole, speaking imprecisely. It's a kind of "Ehrrrm" that accompanies one side of his mouth dipping down slightly, in a look that says "Not quite," or "Not really." It's the sound jodhpurs would make, if they made a sound.

Like my mother, I did have some bravado on board, but I never felt completely comfortable deploying it in an official setting. It seemed a little embarrassing, to take yourself seriously in public the way men did. Who would preen and flaunt their talents like that? As a woman, you could only use your swagger in playful, nonserious contexts, or in private. So my bravado mostly gave me a solid quarters game in college, or it made me prone to break into terrible dance moves when no one was watching. Sometimes my bravado attracted men, but only those sorts of men who were impressed by brash women. My bravado always felt more comfortable with a drink in its hand. My bravado always felt more at home on the printed page than it did live and in person.

My bravado became jittery and indifferent in an office environment. I could do concrete, measurable work, but I didn't want to represent myself in any official way. I was always checking in with my bosses, to make sure that they saw me as capable. I wanted them to measure the amount of concrete work I did. I wanted them to notice that my work was better than other people's work. I wanted them to see how much effort I put in.

Generally speaking, bosses are not fired up to do a careful accounting of their underlings' work. If they were, they wouldn't be bosses in the first place. Most of the time, what bosses respond to is what bosses themselves value the most: bravado. But I never felt right clearing my throat, or telling anyone that their work needed more work. I didn't like to pretend—that I knew more than I actually did, or that I was on board with something that seemed ill-considered. Being a professional seemed to require a lot of pretending. I only wanted to barter in the concrete.

This attitude might've led me down a path to administrative work. But even with administrative jobs, few bosses rewarded the number of concrete tasks you completed each day. Writing, on the other hand, couldn't be more concrete. You write something and turn it in. You make the widgets. Someone pays you for them. Everyone knows exactly how productive you are.

At my first real job as a staff writer, I disdained all of the vague tasks that were impossible to measure: Meetings went on too long, and I felt anxious if I didn't offer any insights that were treated as valuable. I didn't want to simply show my face in the office and punch my time card. I wanted to produce measurable, unimpeachable widgets. So I asked to work remotely, from another city. That way, I could manage my own time. I could be more productive than ever, without a single minute of pointless hot air emanating from me or anyone else.

I've worked from home ever since: twenty years and counting. My husband flies all over the world to give talks and go to academic conferences. I have all of the arrogance and condescension to have become a world-renowned expert, too. But I am a freelance writer instead, so I have a lot of shit to do.

—

Being capable and productive feels somewhat beside the point these days. Either you're popular, and therefore exciting and successful and a winner, or you're unpopular, and therefore unimportant and invisible and devoid of redeeming value. Being capable was much more celebrated in the 1970s when I was growing up. People had real jobs that lasted a lifetime back then, and many workers seemed to embrace the promise that if you worked steadily and capably for years, you would be rewarded for it. Even without those rewards, working hard and knowing how to do things seemed like worthwhile enterprises in themselves.

"Can she bake a cherry pie, Billy Boy, Billy Boy?" my mom

used to sing while rolling out pie crust with her swift, dexterous hands. Sexist as its message may have been, the modern version of that song might be worse. It would center around taking carefully staged and filtered photos of your pretty face next to a piece of cherry pie and posting it to your Instagram account, to be rewarded with two thousand red hearts for your efforts. Making food, tasting it, sharing it, understanding yourself as a human who can do things—all of this is flattened down to nothing, now, since only one or two people would ever know about it. Better to feed two thousand strangers an illusion than engage in real work to limited ends.

My daughter once asked me, "Who is more famous, you or Daddy?" "Neither of us is famous," I replied. I thought about the four copies of my memoir, the one that now costs $6.00 on Amazon, sitting on the bookshelf gathering dust in our bedroom. I thought about my husband's last weeklong trip away from home, the way the kids kept asking me why I never fly anywhere for work like he does. I remembered how my younger daughter used to think I worked at the Coffee Bean, because I always left the house saying I was going to the Coffee Bean "to work." I wished that my daughters had some sense of how hard I work (or at least try to work) every single day. I set the bar high for myself. My work always needs more work. Work that needs more work sounds like one high, thin note that stretches on and on forever.

Thinking about this made me a little peeved at all those swaggering heroes with their trips and their bravado and their fucking jodhpurs. Maybe I limited myself by assuming that men are the ones who are suited to flying around and bloviating, while women are the ones who silently work behind the scenes, hidden from view. Why have I always kept my bravado on the written page or in a glass rattling with ice cubes? Maybe if I could stand in the doorway between my office and the office of a very fast typist who was paid to contribute to my successes, I might be more productive, more imaginative, more willing to reach beyond the safe and familiar, in my work and in my life. I would proceed with direction and purpose, guided by the certainty that this world is mine as much as anyone else's.

My mood shifted. Imagine a dramatic key change, a half step up the scale. Imagine the sound of the shift bar engaging, that sound a typewriter makes when the whole carriage moves up a quarter of an inch and stays there, IN ALL CAPS.

"SURE, DADDY HAS A GREAT JOB," I explained, trying to take the all-caps out of my voice. "HE IS, UM . . . very important in his field. But there are only about three hundred academics around the country who do what he does." I pictured them all, reading and studying each other's work, then flying to conferences to reassure each other of their collective importance. "But when my column comes out, at least fifty thousand people read it. Fifty thousand is a lot more than three hundred."

"That's so many!" my daughter says. "That's like everyone in the world."

"Not really. There are seven billion people in the world. That's a hundred thousand times more than the number of people who read my column."

"Oh. So you're just a little bit famous."

"The word 'famous' doesn't really apply," I said.

Silence. Suspense building.

"But I am more famous than Daddy. Most people would agree with me about that."

The sound of pointless competitiveness, an awkward grab

for glory, is a little bit like a major chord being played sloppily but with great force on a church organ, by a small, angry child.

—

As attention and popularity start to feel more important than ever but also, somehow, cheaper and emptier than ever, maybe it's time for more of us to savor the luxury of remaining mysterious, of staying hidden. Sometimes when I get offered an important-seeming job or speaking gig, I feel like the true gift is not the opportunity itself but the freedom to say no. In a world filthy with flashers, I have trouble grasping the concrete gains of increased exposure.

And maybe some stubborn part of me wants to be the capable one instead of the one who can't remember what day of the week it is. Some sexist part of me thinks that it's better to be the busy, condescending one, at home in her soft pants, talking to the dogs and rolling her eyes when she overhears the arrogant throat-clearing of a Skype conference in the next room, or shoving a pillow over her head when the snoring starts to sound like a minor-key crescendo of jet engines, taking off for Helsinki or Shanghai or Singapore.

But no one should have to choose between becoming a capable, pragmatic handmaiden who tries not to take up too much space and a disorganized dreamer with a bloated ego who steps on everyone's toes. And I can see now that other people have ego rewards built into their daily lives—meetings, conferences, watercooler talk, accolades, long mutually congratulatory conversations with their peers. As shallow as those things can feel, after years of packing my days with as much efficient work as possible and treating any moment of self-satisfaction as shameful, it's about time I gazed at a bookshelf filled with leather-bound journals. I want to be unabashedly

proud of my work for once in my life. I want to hold my ground and acknowledge that I'm an adult now and I know some things. Instead of apologizing for being too proud or insisting that my accomplishments aren't that big of a deal, I want to sigh contentedly as I lean way back in my swivel chair. My sighs will sound like the "Poof!" a wild mushroom makes when you step right into the middle of it for no good reason, other than you're alone in the woods and the woods belong to you for just a moment.

I want that for my daughters—and for everyone else who ever felt small when they heard the sound of a cleared throat, one that announces its right to hold forth before it utters a single word. The capable, the hardworking, those who tackle concrete tasks with stunning efficiency deserve that flavor of bravado. We should all learn to play nicely with others, sure, but not so nicely that we're the ones organizing and scheduling and remembering while some dude gets to wander around, unfocused but still sure of his place in the world. Sometimes when you are good at hard work, you give yourself too much of it. And with too much hard work in front of you, you might not also have the time and space to be truly brilliant.

Brilliance doesn't depend only on talk and flair, even though we're sometimes tempted to believe so. Brilliance depends on believing in the hard work you're capable of doing, but it also depends on believing in your potential, believing in your mind, believing in your heart. Brilliance sometimes relies on believing in your talents before you have any evidence that they're there. What a luxury, to take such an enormous leap of faith, without hesitation!

Because even as I've worked hard year after year for more than twenty years now, as I've polished my work and demanded steady improvement from myself and asked myself to do better, I realize that for all of the concrete skills I've

gained, nothing takes the place of truly believing that my ideas and words have a right to be taken seriously. And if I believed enough in my talents years ago to own them, who knows what I could've created?

Five thousand little red hearts don't mean much compared to that kind of faith in yourself. I want to taste that kind of faith. I want to feel it in my dirty, calloused hands. I want to know I was called to do this. I am building something big and gorgeous. I am at the center. It shouldn't feel embarrassing to say so out loud. I am a symphony orchestra reaching a crescendo: formidable, chilling, irreplaceable.

survival fantasies

n the year 2012, every night before I peeled the plastic seal off a cup of tapioca and watched *The Real Housewives of Beverly Hills* on my big-screen TV, I would read a chapter of *Little House in the Big Woods* to my daughters, who were five and three at the time. For the first few chapters, Pa mostly tramped around in the woods, shooting at things. First Pa shot a deer and smoked the meat. Next he caught a bunch of fish and salted the meat. One lucky day, he wandered up on a bear that was about to eat a pig. He shot the bear, then lugged it home, along with the bonus pig. The family celebrated!

My girls listened in stunned silence, more accustomed to picture books about Fancy Nancy and Olivia (also a pig). They never imagined that Olivia could be carved up and smoked, or that her tail might be considered a treat if fried in lard, or that her bladder might be filled with air and batted around like a ball.

But as we read on about corn husks that doubled as dolls and smoked-meat-strewn attics that doubled as playrooms, their envy of Laura and Mary became palpable, a sentiment I certainly understood. Something in the way the author lingered over the details—the meticulous smoking process, the daylong, harrowing walk into town, the way the dog bristled and growled when predators were afoot—had the power to make hardships sound soothing and delectable. But then, what girl doesn't dream of spending a long, cold winter huddled in a tiny cabin with her staunchly religious parents, nibbling on smoked deer and lard cakes, while panthers and bears and wolves lurk outside the door?

The perverse pleasures of a pastoral narrative like *Little House in the Big Woods,* which was written by Laura Ingalls Wilder in 1932 (it was a precursor to *Little House on the Prairie*), lie in the fantasy it offers about the deeply spiritual benefits of tangling with nature, whether nature takes the shape of swaying oak trees, giant snowdrifts, or hungry predators. The pastoral genre has been around since ancient Greece, but it took a particular hold on the collective consciousness during the Industrial Revolution, when visions of a serene existence in the country were painted in sharp contrast to the indignities of urban life. The literary critic Terry Eagleton explained in *The Guardian* that the pastoral is "largely the creation of town dwellers. It is the myth of those for whom the country is a place to look at rather than live in." What's interesting about *Little House in the Big Woods* in particular, though, is that instead of exalting a leisurely life in the bucolic countryside, it paints hard labor and the constant threat of death in hues that make them seem as relaxing as a trip to a day spa.

Or maybe that's just how it looked from my modern vantage point. Because after Ma and Laura narrowly escaped a run-in with a giant bear and Pa got back from town and played everyone a ditty on his fiddle, my two girls would step over a sea of plastic toys to get to their beds, and I would remove the sealed top from my tapioca and proceed to become agitated over ladies with surgically redesigned bodies who wept an endless river of tears over casual slights. Eleven hours later, I would be pouring my girls' breakfast out of a cereal box and walking them to their respective concrete schoolyards, where they would play with Disney-princess action figures and eat off-brand Oreos at snack time, while I spent my day squinting at a computer screen until my head throbbed in sync with the drumbeat piped into my earbuds. Being stalked by wild panthers sounded sort of refreshing by comparison.

Maybe that's why the pastoral narrative requires such sharp teeth: If all lives include suffering, we'd like to suffer for valid reasons, and not because our supposedly ergonomic chairs make our backs ache, or the apps on our iPhones won't load quickly enough.

—

When it comes to imaginary hardship, nothing quite beats the apocalypse. If you want your dread and angst to feel more romantic and heroic, "This job is slowly killing me" doesn't hold a candle to "This zombie might slowly eat me alive." And sometimes nothing short of an apocalypse will align the world with your fantasies.

Take the sugary, Armageddon-flavored nuggets of NBC's long-forgotten doomsday drama *Revolution*, which aired from 2012 until 2014. Unlike the cautionary tales scripted by visionaries like George Orwell or J. G. Ballard, *Revolution* felt more like a blatant daydream situated halfway between Dungeons

& Dragons and *Real Simple* magazine. After all the lights go out across the globe (and batteries and gas-powered cars stop working, too, somewhat nonsensically), citizens abandon their gadget-driven existences to sharpen machetes, grow sustainable crops, and engage in mixed martial arts combat. Even the show's CGI images of weed-strewn urban landscapes go from haunting to oddly soothing, as flocks of birds fly through the sky and serene agrarian societies spring up in the cul-de-sacs of suburban neighborhoods.

The apocalypse depicted in *Revolution*—like the ones depicted in the *Hunger Games* and *Divergent* books and movies—corrected a myriad of modern injustices, from laziness to sloppy living to overindulgence. For all the heroes' battles with evil soldiers and bandits patrolling the land, it was the pre-blackout, materialistic, digitally fixated society that represented the real dystopia. It took worldwide catastrophe for TV- and iPhone-hypnotized children to morph into the resourceful, hardworking teenagers of their parents' wishful imaginations. In a refreshing return to the brutal laws of natural selection, millionaire Google executives were reduced to awkward, cowardly geeks who stooped over to catch their breath every few minutes. The injustice of high-tech, remote-control weaponry was supplanted by the more egalitarian rigors of hand-to-hand combat. And the handsome, well-muscled teenager at the heart of *Revolution* soon withered into a helpless damsel in distress, sighing and pouting in captivity while his more able-bodied older sister colluded with a loosely knit band of rebel forces to overthrow the local militia and secure his freedom.

Who wouldn't feel a rush of yearning for this simple if somewhat violent existence? The characters' goals were so concrete: Hit the road in search of help or information; subvert your malevolent overlords—local, observable foes, as opposed to the faceless, splintered, omnipresent enemies we face today; hide your firearms and your American flags from evil outside forces. Even romance is more straightforward: Arrows shot from a crossbow at your mutual enemy are so much more direct than a winking emoji.

Although *Revolution* itself wasn't around for long, it foreshadowed a broader interest in savage TV fantasies to come: *Game of Thrones* was the most popular show in the world in 2016, followed by *The Walking Dead*, with *Westworld* in the number four slot. According to Parrot Analytics, which measures ratings, "peer to peer sharing," and "social media chatter," viewers in 2016 wanted to watch (1) brutal thugs vying for the throne as zombie hordes invaded a fantastical land; (2) brutal thugs vying for food, weapons, and a safe place to hide as zombie hordes invaded the United States; and (3) robots navigating a savage fantasy world created by their brutal thug overlords.

Three out of four of our favorite shows, in other words, were dystopian visions of survival of the most merciless, characterized by extreme isolation from centralized government and mass culture. If anything, *Revolution* wasn't bleak or frightening enough to satisfy our true desires. We craved a forbidding landscape where a gaggle of survivors would be forced to work together to ward off a blind, murderous horde.

This is where our modern obsession with survivalism parts ways with the pastoral strains of Laura Ingalls Wilder: Instead of peacefully coexisting, the heroes of today's wishful dystopias struggle to cooperate with each other under duress. Someone is always trying to undermine or overpower you. Someone has a hidden agenda or a secret disease or a nefarious secret plan. Someone is actually a zombie or a robot. Someone has two dragons in the basement and she's not afraid to use them. Someone has a baseball bat covered with barbed wire that he could whip out without warning.

Even though the dirty work of slicing up zombies or blowing the religious zealots of King's Landing to high heaven is much darker than the high-fiving Mickey Mouse Club patriotism of *Revolution,* the escapist fantasy is roughly the same. When the filthy survivors of *The Walking Dead* discovered a gorgeous old farmhouse, the story echoed similar plotlines in *Looper* and *Signs* and countless other films intent on toying with our idealized notions about the romantic comforts of the heartland. What better place for our heroes to restore their strength, reassert their core values—hell, even fall in love with a farmer's daughter?

But even when our dark fantasies remind us of the perils of collaborating with human beings in real time, face-to-face, to ensure our survival—something that, by all appearances, is far more difficult than the "peer to peer sharing" and "social media chatter" that typify our modern means of engagement—somehow, we're hooked. We savor the notion of crouching in a filthy basement with a complete stranger from two towns over, eating dusty cans of soup and telling old stories, and then smearing zombie blood on our faces to survive the next invasion. We seem to treasure the idea of joining forces with people we would have no reason to talk to in our normal lives—defensive sheriffs and clairvoyant disabled children and women with Japanese sword fetishes and serene ranchers' daughters who are actually very fierce and serene ranchers' daughters who are actually robots. We relish the thought of forming a fragile alliance with a woman who has a way with dragons. We like to imagine almost being sliced to pieces then running like hell then hiding in the dark then crawling through the muck with an angry middle-aged domestic abuse survivor or a flinty bastard son dressed in bearskins or a dignified lady knight with an unflagging sense of loyalty that rarely serves her well as the world is falling to pieces.

—

It's not as if our viewing appetites represent a previously unheard-of strain of fantasy. The authors of apocalyptic fiction have always managed to transform their worst-case scenarios into wish fulfillment. In *Zone One*, Colson Whitehead empties New York City of its bustling crowds, leaving our protagonist to explore the streets and apartments and offices of the city unfettered—which sounds like something Whitehead, who's written passionately about the city, would love to do. In *The Dog Stars*, Peter Heller places his protagonist against a calm, almost idyllic post-end-times landscape with access to his own plane and his own vast stretch of territory—the perfect scenario for an outdoor adventurer like Heller—then drops in an Amazonian female survivor like a care package from the *Maxim* gods. Cormac McCarthy's *The Road* might at first appear bereft of wishful thinking. But for McCarthy, the end times present the ultimate backdrop for contemplating mortality, far more eerie and unsettling than either the scrabbly West or the Appalachian wilds. Here, among the cannibals and the drifting ashes, his stark, biblical prose can take on divine proportions.

The focus of these novels isn't on the shape and form of the catastrophe; those details are often vague, and all of the action there lies in the past. The apocalypse mostly serves as a way to turn up the contrast on a hero's solitary battle to adapt. Stripping away the complications and distractions of the modern world, what does our protagonist have left? The same melancholy and longing he or she always had, of course.

But now there's no need to inject desperation, romance, solitude, or morbidity into such a tale; these qualities are encoded in the apocalyptic novel's DNA, minimizing the trivial clutter and heightening the stakes. Values and ideas about morality are stripped down to their essential nature: Kill or be killed? Conform and tolerate oppression or escape and risk death?

Even in older works like Ballard's *The Drowned World*, such disturbing questions are savored and relished like two-year-old Pop-Tarts scavenged from a stranger's kitchen. There's an obvious delight taken in the awfulness of the transformed planet. In his survey of science fiction, *Billion Year Spree*, Brian Aldiss refers to this tendency of authors to concoct enviable end-times as "the cozy catastrophe." As others suffer and die around him, our hero runs wild, enjoying the fruits of worldwide holocaust.

In most of these apocalyptic tales, whether they're books or movies or TV shows, we find a recurring desire for simplicity and solitude, for a reconnection with the self and the land, for a private chance to determine what one needs to survive and what can be left behind. The characters rarely choose to join a large community and cooperate peacefully within its boundaries and bylaws for the common good. Because as long as it's all fantasy, why subject yourself to the same compromises and restrictions you tolerate in real life? What kind of an imaginative exercise is that? We don't crave the adventures of an optimistic team player. What we want is something that the mandatory optimism and go-get-'em attitude of American culture can't give us. We want a guilt-free escape into struggle and compromise and curmudgeonly solitude. We want a chance to understand our bare minimum requirements for survival. And underneath almost every tale, we discover the same notion: that we might be happier—or at least stronger, more focused, more admirable—if only we had much less.

—

Perhaps the willful act of hara-kiri that most white American voters inflicted on themselves on November 8, 2016, was the logical end point of these desires. It was as if many Americans preferred to step off a tall cliff rather than live with the impermeable blank nothingness and precariousness of modern life. Did the passivity of our screen-led lives slowly transform us into nihilists without our noticing? Because post-election polls indicated that many voters believed that anything was better than where we had landed in 2016. And some voters seemed to crave a legitimate crisis instead of an imaginary one. People wanted "change"—whatever that was—even if the person promising change seemed capable of burning down the world by accident in his fumbled attempts to bring it.

Donald Trump certainly recognized that "change" didn't have to mean anything concrete. It could simply mean that things were about to get unhinged and unpredictable in the manner of reality TV finales. This was the destiny that Neil Postman had predicted back in 1985 in his popular polemic *Amusing Ourselves to Death:* The shift from the nuances of the page and complexity of real life to the blathering incoherence of the TV screen was complete. All that mattered was that our leader continued to build suspense: Each new day, some perceived crime had just been committed, and someone was going to pay for it.

"It's such an exciting time to be an American," Gwyneth Paltrow told a crowd at the Airbnb Open conference in Los Angeles days after the election, according to the *New York Post,* thereby casually manifesting Postman's dark vision of the future with all the blithe cheer of a bored audience member finally getting the big finale she deserves. "[W]e are at this amazing inflection point," Paltrow said. "People are clearly tired of the status quo, and . . . it's sort of like someone threw it all in the air and we're going to see how it all lands." Those with nothing to lose, in other words, welcomed our new insect overlords.

"Some people feel Donald Trump will bring the revolution immediately; if he gets in then things will really explode," a smiling Susan Sarandon told Chris Hayes in March 2016, anticipating bloodshed and upheaval as if it were a particularly thrilling episode of *Game of Thrones*. A few weeks later, Sarandon warned the populace that Hillary Clinton was more dangerous than Donald Trump.

A few months after the election, when asked if she regretted her words, Sarandon refused to apologize, telling Hayes, "What we have now is a populace that is awake." Presumably she was not referring to the people of color and Muslims and immigrants and Jews lying awake at night wondering how to protect themselves and their families from a president taking his cues from a militant horde of white supremacists, anti-Semites, and anti-immigration zealots. "Seriously, I'm not worried about a wall being built and Mexico paying for it," Sarandon continued. "He's not going to get rid of every Muslim living in this country."

Other Americans seemed a little more worried than Sarandon was. Black Americans did not seem confused about how Trump's refusal to condemn Nazis and white supremacists throughout his campaign might predict his attitudes and policy choices as president. Likewise, many immigrants and LGBTQ people, who'd experienced hatred and prejudice firsthand, appeared to recognize the dire consequences of electing a populist firebrand who knew how to use ignorance, hatred, and bigotry to his advantage.

But a vast swath of white Americans seemed more in touch with some fantasy in their heads than they were with reality.

At least this way, something exciting will happen, they seemed to say. The dragons always save the good ones, after all. Those abandoned cupboards are always filled with cans of edible food. The bastard son in bearskins always arrives just in the nick of time.

—

A blonde woman in a hot pink spandex tank hoists a sledge-hammer over her shoulders, then slams it down with a dull thud onto the big tire in front of her. Beside her, another woman swings her sledgehammer even higher, grimacing and groaning with the effort. Their faces are bright red and drip-ping with sweat. It's 9:45 a.m. and eighty-five degrees outside, and the sun is glinting off the asphalt of the strip-mall parking lot where the women are laboring. "Swing it higher, above your shoulder!" a woman bellows at them, even as they gasp each time they raise their hammers, each time they let them fall.

As one woman pauses to wipe the sweat from her eyes, she spots me studying her. I've been trying not to stare, but it's a strange spectacle, this John Henry workout of theirs, hammer-ing away in front of a women's fitness center, just a few doors down from a smoke shop and a hair salon. It looks exhausting, and more than a little dangerous. (What if a sledgehammer slips and flies from one woman's hands, braining her compan-ion?) It also looks pointless. Why not join a roofing crew for a few hours instead? Surely, there's a tunnel somewhere that needs digging, or at least some hot tar that needs pouring.

But paying to simulate backbreaking labor under the watch-ful eye of a demanding authority figure seems to be a common desire in the land of the free. When I type "sledgehammer" into Google later that day, the first suggestion is "sledgehammer workout," a search term that pours forth half a dozen enthusiastic reenactments of life on a steel-driving chain gang.

Fitness culture couldn't have changed more dramatically since the late 1960s. Back then, residents of my small Southern hometown would spot my father, an early jogger, and yell out of their car windows, "Keep running, hippie!" These days there aren't that many joggers in my Los Angeles neighborhood, but every other block there's another fitness center offering boot-camp classes or Brazilian jujitsu, with people inside punching, kicking, and yelling at one another like drill sergeants. Jim Fixx's freewheeling running disciples have been replaced by packs of would-be Navy SEALs, sprinting up sandy hillsides with backpacks full of rocks strapped to their shoulders.

Jane Fonda and Richard Simmons once painted exercise as something fun and faintly sexy—a lighthearted trip to a sweaty nightclub in your own living room—but fitness today isn't supposed to be easy. The "Abdomenizer" and "8-Minute Abs" videos, which practically suggested that exercise could be squeezed in between bites of your hamburger, are now quaint punch lines. By the 1990s, when the soft curves of Ursula Andress had been replaced by the hard bodies of Cindy Crawford and Elle Macpherson, you worked out to prepare for the beach or the bedroom. These days, though, you aren't preparing for fun or romance. You're preparing for an unforeseen natural disaster, or a burning building, or Armageddon.

"We have sought to build a program that will best prepare trainees for any physical contingency—not only for the unknown, but for the unknowable." This dark talk passes for welcoming language on the website of CrossFit, the intense, ultracompetitive conditioning program whose motto, "Forging Elite Fitness," reflects our current fascination with both elite athletes and elite military forces. In spite of (or because of) the fact that CrossFit is now nearly synonymous with over-exertion, there are more than six thousand affiliates in the United States.

Those stunned by CrossFit's popularity are often surprised, given its high price, to discover its spartan ethos: Each "box" (its lingo for gym) is usually just a big empty room with medicine balls, barbells, and wooden boxes stacked along the walls. Workouts rotate daily but tend to involve free weights, sprints, and squats. In keeping with its apocalyptic mission statement, the program encourages camaraderie under duress (Cross-Fitters coach each other through the pain) and competition (names and scores are scrawled on a wipe board and sometimes posted online).

Despite the risks inherent to hundreds of thousands of people dabbling in Olympic weight-lifting techniques at their local strip malls, CrossFitters seem utterly dedicated to their hardcore workouts. CrossFit's founder, Greg Glassman, admitted in 2005 that rhabdomyolysis—a dangerous condition that can lead to kidney failure—had popped up among a few new CrossFit converts. He viewed it, in part, as evidence of Cross-Fit's "dominance over traditional training protocols." Crucially, this type of conditioning was important not just for body tone but also for responding to calamity. "Nature, combat and emergency can demand high volumes of work performed quickly for success or for survival," Glassman wrote. "Until others join CrossFit in preparing athletes for this reality, the exertional rhabdo problem will be ours to shoulder alone." The ideal world, in other words, is populated by pumped-up gladiators, prepared for whatever battle the future might hold. The path to this world is necessarily lined with ER visits.

CrossFitters represent just one wave of a fitness sea change, in which well-to-do Americans abandon easy, convenient forms of exercise in favor of workouts grueling enough to resemble a kind of physical atonement. For the most privileged among us, freedom seems to oppress, and oppression feels like a kind of freedom.

The whole notion of pushing your physical limits—popularized by early Nike ads, Navy SEAL mythos, and Lance Armstrong's cult of personality—has attained a religiosity that's as passionate as it is pervasive. The "extreme" version of anything is now widely assumed to be an improvement on the original, rather than a perverse amplification of it. And as with most of sports culture, there is no gray area. You win or you lose. You leave it all on the floor—or you shamefully skulk off the floor with extra gas in your tank.

Our new religion has more than a little in common with the religions that brought our ancestors to America in the first place. Like the idealists and extremists who founded this country, the modern zealots of exercise turn their backs on the indulgences of our culture, seeking solace in self-abnegation and suffering. "This is the route to a better life," they tell us, gesturing at their sledgehammers and their kettlebells, their military drills and their startling reenactments of hard labor. And in uncertain times, it doesn't sound so bad to be prepared for some coming disaster.

This sort of twisted logic permeated my thoughts as I read *Little House in the Big Woods* to my kids a few years back. As I ran on the treadmill at the gym, I wondered: Wouldn't it be better if I were breaking a sweat not from running on this hamster wheel but from disarticulating a bear? Wouldn't I be more serene if I spent my days pickling beets or hunching over a laundry pail? And shouldn't my children be right here with me, sewing on their nine-patch quilts? Wouldn't we all be happier if we spent our time together, just us and no one else, learning about what's really important, never getting distracted by what isn't? The fantasy enabled by *Little House in the Big Woods* goes beyond the pastoral's focus on communion with nature and with your own instincts or even with the satisfaction of muscles that ache from a day of hard work. At its heart, *Little House* is a fantasy of total isolation and total control.

It's no wonder, then, that some of the most memorable scenes in the *Little House* series focus on temporary relief from that isolation—when, for instance, Laura and Ma and Pa and the other townspeople join together in the church to sing songs and give thanks to God for His blessings. From that vantage point, we might see CrossFit not only as a Darwinian ode to individual survival, but also as a kind of communion— a worship that includes suffering and sweating together with the drill sergeant as our new preacher.

For today's privileged, maybe the most grueling path seems like the one most likely to lead to divinity. When I run on Sunday mornings, I pass seven fitness boutiques, packed and bustling, and five nearly empty churches.

—

If Laura Ingalls Wilder's nostalgic tour through a simpler time has a modern equivalent, it's *The Pioneer Woman*, the personal blog of Ree Drummond, who traded in her shallow big-city existence for life on an Oklahoma ranch. It takes only a few minutes of voyeuristically perusing Drummond's pastoral pleasure dome, with its gorgeous photographs of Drummond cooking dinner for her family or homeschooling her four tow-headed children, to realize that you are a failure. Gazing at photos of Drummond's kids riding their horses under a cloud-dappled Maxfield Parrish sky, you remember the mac and cheese from a box you fed your kids as they begged to watch the latest Lady Gaga video on your laptop. Drummond fries chicken and teaches her children algebra and shakes her luscious mane of red hair in the Oklahoma sunshine, and her pioneer children dream of tornadoes and prairie grass and lassoing cows. Your kids dream of *Kung Fu Panda 2* and Space Mountain and frozen yogurt covered in gummi bears.

But the best pages of *The Pioneer Woman* concern Drummond's husband, who is a cowboy and therefore wears a cowboy hat and leather chaps, just like that guy from the Village People. Seemingly aware that her husband's entire life is an elaborate, semi-pornographic work of performance art derived from pop images of the American West, Drummond refers to him as Marlboro Man and shoots photographs of him wearing ten-gallon hats, propping his cowboy boots on metal gates, and squinting grittily into the midday sun. Under these photographs she writes captions that land somewhere between William Carlos Williams and *Playgirl:* "My husband. He's still waiting on the calves. And wearing a vest. And lighting my fire." Elsewhere she writes, "He's rugged and virile," apparently prepping his dossier for his next national Chippendales tour.

But the core of Marlboro Man's appeal—like Pioneer Woman's, and Ma and Pa's before them—rests in this blurry backdrop of toil under pressure from the ever-changing seasons. Alongside the gorgeous photographs of windblown prairies and luminous skies and dinner tables arranged for twenty, there are allusions to reading lessons and vaccinating calves and doing five loads of laundry every day. Even though readers are well aware that *The Pioneer Woman* may not be a portal into a simpler, better life so much as a carefully art-directed, commercially sponsored fantasy, we are happy to suspend our disbelief. We watch Drummond shilling for Babycakes Mini Treat Makers and shooting spots on the *Today* show and wrapping her cooking show for the Food Network, even as her blog, registering more than twenty million page views per month, outlines a life of unending hard work—of home-schooling and cooking and housework.

Drummond offers up a nostalgic vision of hard work in isolation far from the bleakness of urban life, with its concrete playgrounds and indifferent teachers and blind institutions. With *The Pioneer Woman,* our urban and suburban indignities dissolve into a haze of homemade doughnuts and pretty sunsets and a house packed with doting mothers-in-law and uncles and cousins.

—

When Jedediah Purdy, a homeschooled twenty-four-year-old from rural West Virginia, wrote *For Common Things,* his best-selling paean to agrarian living and homeschooling, back in 1999, he was mostly encountered as an outlier. But after the tragic turns of the past two decades—Enron, Katrina, 9/11, the banking crisis, the recession, Puerto Rico, the Las Vegas massacre—it's easy for modern civic life to appear as rotten as it did during the Industrial Revolution. The resultant surge in homeschooling and urban homesteading and home births and other laborious efforts at self-sufficiency make Purdy's writing look prescient today.

While so many aspects of the green movement—farmers' markets, composting, gray water, solar power—represent commendable efforts to improve life within a community, there's a spirit of separatism that can't be disentangled from these things. The allure of hard work and self-reliance, when paired with a distrust for modern institutions, can curdle into an impulse to divest from society altogether. Whether this impulse is manifested in the suspicions of disaster preppers or the purism of the homeschooler, there's a sense that the more independent you are, the safer you are, that total control of our environments is the ideal, and that the institutions designed to protect us might be those from which we require protection.

But our fear of the "other" is also more mundane than that. It's a way of choosing the inconveniences of self-reliance over the indignities and sacrifices of compromise. Perhaps it's better (this thinking goes) to acquire the skills to face down a hungry bear in the woods or trudge through the snow to buy a few bolts of calico than it is to expose your child to a teacher who doesn't inspire her, or to a doctor who doesn't listen closely enough. That's a pastoral fantasy that easily overshadows our hunched, bleary-eyed, flickering-screen lives—but the fantasy is also a product of those lives, which create awkwardness and fear of direct confrontation in a population unaccustomed to face-to-face contact, accommodation, and collaboration.

But most of all, this dream of purity and separation feeds the delusion that isolation is the most honorable choice, that dropping out is somehow more valiant than working slowly to reform the system and help those who are truly in need. Sometimes hope doesn't offer the same sense of comfort that closing the cabin doors does.

"The poet is in command of his fantasy," Lionel Trilling wrote, "while it is exactly the mark of the neurotic that he is possessed by his fantasy." The modern mind, twitchy and inconstant, is a fertile ground for neuroticism and for fantasy. But the absolutism of fantasy has a way of snuffing out initiative: If your life pales compared to the gossamer lifestyle fairy tale, why aspire to more? Conversely, if the end of the world sounds oddly alluring, why fight it?

Ultimately, though, it's arrogant to imagine that going it alone is any nobler than collaborating, compromising, working within a community in order to improve it. We need each other to survive the catastrophes to come. But more importantly, we need each other to prevent them.

true romance

As an advice columnist, I sometimes get asked how people can "keep the romance alive" in their marriages. This stumps me a little because, by "romance," I know they mean the traditional version, the one that depends on living inside a giant, suspenseful question mark. This version of romance focuses on that thrilling moment when you believe you've met someone who might make every single thing in the world feel delicious and amazing and right, forever and ever. The romance itself springs forth from big questions: "Can *this* really be what I've been looking for? Will I *really* feel loved and desired and truly adored at last? Can I finally be seen as the answer to someone else's dream, the heroine with the glimmering eyes and sultry smile?" This version of romance peaks at the exact moment when you think, "Holy Christ, I really *am* going to melt right into this other person (who is a relative stranger)! It really *is* physically intoxicating and perfect! And it seems like we feel the exact same way about each other!"

Traditional romance is heady and exciting precisely because— and not in spite of the fact that—there are other, more insidious questions lingering at the edges of the frame: "Will I be enough? Will you be enough? Will we be enough together?"

But once you've been married for a long time, a whole new flavor of romance takes over. It's not the romance of rom-coms, which are predicated on the question of "Will this person really love me (which seems impossible), or does this person actually hate me (which seems far more likely)?" And it's not the romance of watching someone's every move like a stalker, and wanting to lick his face but trying to restrain yourself. It's not even the romance of "Whoa, you bought me flowers, you must *really* love me!" or "Wow, look at us here, as the sun sets, your lips on mine, we really are doing this love thing!" That's dating romance, newlywed romance. You're still pinching yourself. You're still fixated on whether or not it's really happening. You're still kind of, sort of looking for *proof.* The little moments of validation bring the romance.

But after many years of marriage, you don't *need* any more proof. What you have instead—and what I would argue is the most deeply romantic thing of all—is this palpable, reassuring sense that it's okay to be a human being. Because until you feel absolutely sure that you won't eventually be abandoned, it's maybe not 100 percent clear that any other human mortal can tolerate another human mortal. The smells. The sounds. The repetitive fixations on the same nonsense, over and over. Even as you develop a kind of a resigned glaze of *oh, this again* in, say, marital years one through five, you also feel faintly unnerved by your own terrible mortal humanness.

Or you should feel that way.

For example: I talk to my dogs. A lot. My husband does not comment on how much I do this. I am a true dog lady, but one who also has a husband and kids around. While the dog lady has a long conversation with her dogs, the husband and kids are the ones who stand by, cocking their heads quizzically, trying to understand. When I walk in the door after being gone all day, I greet the dogs first. I say things like, "Oh, did you miss your mommy? Oh, you missed your mommy a lot! You needed Mommy but Mommy wasn't here! Poor puppies!" Then I say things to my kids like, "Hey. What's up." There's a tonal shift; I am less enthusiastic, possibly because I'm unwell. My kids don't seem to mind. It takes me longer to warm up and cuddle with them, possibly because they're sometimes whining or yelling about something, or asking hard questions about playdates with kids I don't like, and I can't answer their questions until I take my shoes off like Mr. Rogers and lie prone for a few minutes and pour beer into my face.

That's when I notice my husband. He missed Mommy, too.

But my husband doesn't yell *what the hell?* at me like he could. He doesn't sneer. He doesn't roll his eyes. I am clearly unwell, but he makes no sounds to this effect. Instead, he hugs me and smiles and says, "How was your day, baby?" He acts like he doesn't even notice that I should be locked away forever and ever in some bad, drafty place that serves only American cheese.

And now I'm going to tell you the most romantic story of all. I was very sick out of the blue with some form of dysentery. It hit overnight. I got up to go to the bathroom, and I fainted on the way and cracked my ribs on the side of the bathtub. My husband discovered me there, passed out, in a scene that . . . well, imagine what would happen if you let Todd Solondz direct an episode of *Game of Thrones*. Think about what that might look like. I'm going to take your delicate sensibilities into account and resist the urge to paint a clearer picture for you.

My husband was not happy about this scene. But he handled it without complaint. That is the very definition of romance: not only *not* being made to feel crappy about things that are clearly out of your control, but being quietly cared for by someone who can shut up and do what needs to be done under duress. That is the definition of sexy, too. People think they want a cowboy, because cowboys are rugged and macho and they don't whine. But almost anyone can ride a stallion across a beautiful prairie and then come home and eat a giant home-cooked steak without whining about it. Bravely entering into a wretched dysentery scene, though, will try the most stalwart and unflinching souls among us.

Now let's tackle something even darker and more unpleasant, the seeming antithesis of our modern notion of romance: Someone is dying in their own bed, and someone's spouse is sitting at the bedside, holding the dying person's hand, and also handling all kinds of unspeakable things that people who aren't drowning in gigantic piles of cash sometimes have to handle all by themselves. To me, that's romance. Romance is surviving and then not surviving anymore, without being ashamed of any of it.

Because survival is ugly. Survival means sometimes smelling and sounding the wrong way. It's one thing for a person to buy you flowers, to purchase a nice dinner, to *prove* that they truly, deeply want to have some good sweet-talky time and some touching time alone with you, and maybe they'd like to do that whole routine forever and ever and ever. That's a heady thing. You might imagine eating out at nice restaurants and screwing, and eating out and screwing and eating out and screwing. Romance, in this view, is like Bill Murray in *Groundhog Day,* except he's repeating the same sexily suspenseful moment over and over again.

True romance, though, is more like the movie *True Romance:* Two deluded, lazy people face a bewildering sea of filth and blood and gore together, but they make it through it all somehow without losing their minds completely.

Because it's one thing to savor the complex flavor profiles of expensive meals together. But it's another thing entirely for a human being to listen to you try to figure out how the day went for your dogs, who cannot speak English or any other human language. ("Was it hard, being without Mommy? Yes, I think it was! I think you needed your mommy, but she wasn't here!") And it's another thing entirely when you start to grow an alien in your belly, a process that renders you sharp-tongued and menacing, and then one day the alien finally comes out, all covered in white slime. That is next-level romance right there! And suddenly, all you do is talk to the hairless alien and feed it with your own body (a miracle!), bragging about how you make food from thin air like a GOD, and then, once the alien goes to bed, you say *Jesus I'm exhausted* and *ouch my boobs hurt* and then you pass out in a smelly, unattractive heap. And once you have kids, even in a first-world country, you enter a kind of simulation of third-world living. You're feeding one kid with your body while your husband crouches on the floor of a dressing room at the mall, wiping excrement off the other kid's butt. You and your spouse are slogging through the slop of survival together.

And it's romantic. Mark my words.

You're not alone together very often, and when you are, you sometimes forget how to talk like adults, how to form words about your experiences. You feel more like two herd animals bumping along, all blank stares and pensive chewing. But it's romantic how you both have no thoughts in your heads whatsoever.

The years go by, and it gets less desperate. You get sick less often because you don't wake up fifteen times a night. There's less fecal matter to wipe up, and less grizzly-bear-mother rage at the ready. But now you're getting older, so you say things like "Goddamn my ass hurts." That is also romantic! It makes you both chuckle. You are both mortal and you're both surviving, together, and you're in this until the very end. You are both screwed, everything will be exactly this unexciting until one of you dies, and it's the absolute greatest anyway.

So don't let anyone tell you that marriage is comfortable and comforting but not romantic. Don't let anyone tell you that living and dying together is some sad dance of codependent resignation. Our dumb culture tricks us into believing that romance is the suspense of not knowing whether someone loves you or not yet; the suspense of wanting to have sex but not being able to yet; the suspense of wanting all problems and puzzles to be solved by one person without knowing whether or not that person has any particular affinity for puzzles yet. We think romance is a mystery in which you add up clues that you will be loved. Romance must be carefully staged and art-directed, so everyone looks better than they usually do and seems sexier than they actually are, so the suspense can remain intact.

You are not better than you are, though, and neither is your partner. *That* is romance. Laughing at how beaten down you sometimes are, in your tireless quest to survive, is romance. It's sexy to feel less than totally sexy and still feel like you're sexy to one person, no matter what. Maybe suspense yields to the suspension of disbelief. Maybe looking for proof yields to finding new ways to muddle through the messes together.

But when it's 10:00 p.m. and you crawl into bed like two

old people and tell each other about the weird things that your kids said that day and crack stupid jokes and giggle and then maybe you feel like making out or maybe you just feel like playing a quick game of Candy Crush, all the while saying things like "This game is stupid, it sucks" and "Your feet are freezing" and "My ass hurts"—that's romantic. Because at some point, let's be honest, death supplies the suspense. *How long can this glorious thing last?* your eyes sometimes seem to ask each other. You, for one, really hope this lasts a whole hell of a lot longer. You savor the repetitive, deliciously mundane rhythms of survival, and you want to keep surviving. You want to muddle through the messiness of life together as long as you possibly can. That is the summit. Savor it. That is the very definition of romance.

a scourge of gurus

When the gurus on your block outnumber the tradespeople or teachers or artists, surely that's a sign that the world has lost its footing. Because even as the guru seduces you with his wicked poetry of self-actualization, each lesson is filthy with reminders of your relative shortcomings. There is always the faintest hint that you haven't arrived yet, that you can and should do better, and that if you fail, you deserve your fate. There is always the not-so-subtle implication that you have already squandered your gifts and will continue to do so until you learn to exert control over every dimension of your existence. But if you do somehow manage to rise above your current circumstances, there will be no more suffering or second-guessing, no more rage or injustice, and the bounty of the earth will be yours to plunder. The guru's words are haunted by the looming shadow of your so-called best life, an implicit rejection of the life you're living right now.

The guru is not an expert in happiness or inner peace, although he plays one on the internet. He is not a role model in the realm of fighting injustice or saving the world from disease or throwing his body onto the battlefield. He is a champion of the self. His livelihood relies not only on the defeat of human emotions, but on a denial of the existence of prejudice, of resistance, of the machinery of oppression, of the impenetrable forces that maintain the status quo, of the ever-widening gap between rich and poor, of the disastrously callous habits of the overclass and the bought-out legislators who serve them. The guru will not instruct you on how to navigate a world that distrusts or despises you, nor will he acknowledge that the landscape you inhabit was built to keep you poor, powerless, and suspect.

In other words, the guru is an expert at gaming privilege. Many of his so-called life hacks are just that, *hacks*—sly methods of disrupting other people's resources for the sake of your own. If you happen to have a few demographic advantages, plus the raw self-loathing and lack of affection for humanity that tend to accompany any sustained imperative to maximize your own delicious supremacy behind fortress walls, the guru can make you king or queen of all that you survey. Everyone else can, of course, get fucked.

—

Wildly popular guru Timothy Ferriss is undoubtedly a smart, driven human being with countless helpful tips on how neurotic slackers trussed up in business casual like himself can jimmy the locks on the realm of the elite. Even though Ferriss's publishing success began with that paean to lazy privilege and its spoils *The 4-Hour Workweek,* then moved on to interval training, "increasing fat-loss 300%," and inciting "The 15-Minute Female Orgasm" in *The 4-Hour Body,* he has since broadened his appeal to gather wisdom from an unwieldy gaggle of tech CEOs, chess masters, athletes, hedge fund managers, poker players, and a few fellow gurus. In his new book, *Tribe of Mentors: Short Life Advice from the Best in the World,* Ferriss fires the same eleven questions at each of his "mentors," and their answers—short or long, concise or rambling—are printed and sold (with Ferriss, we can safely assume, pocketing the profits). A similar harvesting occurs on his podcast, *The Tim Ferriss Show,* which often features guests holding forth at length with no interruptions from our host, calling to mind a hastily prepared TedX Talk or a not very well-produced infomercial. Like Ferriss's blog and podcast, much of the material in *Tribe of Mentors* focuses on pragmatic methods of "extracting your max" (as a language-slaughtering guru might put it): "What purchase of $100 or less has most positively impacted your life?"; "In the last five years, what new belief, behavior, or habit has most improved your life?"; "What is an unusual habit or an absurd thing that you love?"; "How has a failure, or apparent failure, set you up for success?"

But whether Ferriss's mentors answer questions about what message they would write on a giant billboard or what advice they'd give to college students about to enter the "real world," they can't help to conjure the same self-optimizing flavor of Timothy Ferriss himself. Even when they sing the praises of meditation or richer connections with others or fighting for a better planet, like all Ferriss-branded content, their words boil down to the same quest: to minimize the tedious hassles of survival so you can spend more of your time flying first-class to surf spots around the globe with similarly enlightened extreme athletes and tech bros.

"Greatness is not a final destination," Maurice Ashley, the chess master, author, and ESPN commentator, advises *Tribe* readers, "but a series of small acts done daily in order to constantly rejuvenate and refresh our skills in [an] effort to become a better version of ourselves." "When I am feeling unfocused, the first question I ask myself is, 'Am I rehearsing my best self?'" offers Adam Robinson, cofounder of the Princeton Review, "And if the answer is no, I ask myself how can I reset." "Social media works best when you provide massive value. I paid attention to analytics (likes, dislikes, views, etc.) and curbed my postings to fit what was trending (what was most valuable)," says Jon Call, who has apparently leveraged this approach to secure a career as an "anabolic acrobat."

For hundreds of pages, we encounter a vast range of secrets and tips and suggestions, some of them useful (Chef Eric Ripert advocates "altruistic actions" and "being mindful of others" as the way to true inner happiness), others less so (Call recommends the use of smelling salts when you "can't get your mind off sex and have no way to release"). But somehow after perusing advice about eliminating inefficient meetings and the futility of endurance cardio and the importance of good personality tests for evaluating hires, it's hard to ignore how many of these "mentors" were selected in Ferriss's image. Even if they care deeply about solving the world's ills, they repeatedly return most enthusiastically to enhancing the self, as if the self were a stock portfolio that needed better diversification.

After a while, it's hard to avoid the sensation that many of Ferriss's mentors are the sorts of people who read *Zen and the Art of Motorcycle Maintenance* over and over again but never read other works of fiction or essays or even the morning paper. Their recommendations are often so abstract, yet so devoid of any evidence of real struggle or adversity, that it's difficult not to imagine a tech CEO with artistic photographs of Martin Luther King, Jr., on his walls who, nonetheless, isn't completely sure what the point of Black Lives Matter is. There is a lot of quoting Viktor Frankl's *Man's Search for Meaning* but a notable absence of any attempt to address the real-life nazis outside our doors.

But maybe that's just how warped their intentions become when their words are curated by Ferriss—or by whichever stooge he's outsourced for such tedium while he's either sampling the fine wines of the world or retaking his own 30-Day No Booze No Masturbating Challenge. The demonic shadow of your best life that haunts everything Timothy Ferriss touches, in other words, is actually *Timothy Ferriss's* best life.

This is why, on each page, instead of reaching for some higher realm of consciousness, we seem to be reminded of the oddly bland but hopelessly macho hustle this Übermensch has managed to pull off, day after day. But isn't that the true mark of the successful guru? His sole aim is to become an unimpeachable brand with a central message that boils down to no message at all. Any real, substantive message—political or emotional or philosophical—would only expose him to disapproval. Instead, what the guru stands for is simple greatness, bestness, aspiration itself. This is why we're so often treated to photos of Ferriss online posing with Jamie Foxx, Laird Hamilton, or Arnold Schwarzenegger, and offered footage of all of his megarich and powerful bromances.

Considering the large volume of Timothy-Ferriss-branded material currently in circulation, we know relatively little about Ferriss's inner life, his struggles, his emotional connection to what he creates. We rarely hear about his politics, or whether he's depressed or energized by the state of the world. We know enough to grok that his friendships often double as cobranding opportunities and his most heartfelt sentiments often double as marketing messages. And we know that, instead of being suspicious of those who never share their wealth or their energy with the poor or the oppressed, Ferriss is suspicious of those who haven't professed loyalty to his brand. In one episode of his podcast, he brings up another fitness guru, adding, "He may or may not be a fan of my stuff. He's not a fan of a lot of people. But that's fine. I'm okay with it. Because even if he doesn't like me, I think he's a good resource for intermittent fasting." He has inadvertently revealed his default operating system: Swear fealty to my brand and only then might I consider doing the same for yours.

But what is the point of all of this maximized, optimal, highly efficient, connected, charismatic *effectiveness*? If Ferriss himself is any indication, it's to be a cipher that stands for nothing beyond success itself, a brand that touts its best-seller status like a street barker, that boosts itself on the shoulders of other such brands, that throws a never-ending party for itself. Like his guru ilk, Ferriss manages to be invisible, efficient, and enviable, without daring to be honorable or righteous or admirable. He is, in other words, the ultimate American hero, the Greatest of Gatsbys, an evanescent tech-bro heartthrob, an emperor with no face. If his bibles for better living could be reduced to a single phrase, it would be: "Become less human."

This goes back to the core religion of the guru, of course: More than anything else, the modern guru denies the existence of external obstacles. Racism, systemic bias, income inequality—to acknowledge these would be to deny the power of the self. They are sidestepped in favor of handy modern conveniences, or the importance of casting off draining relationships, or the constant quest to say no to the countless opportunities rolling your way. What an indulgence it must be, to have your greatest obstacles be "sugar" or "anger" or "toxins."

In many ways, the artist might be seen as the polar opposite of the guru. The artist (or at least some imaginary ideal of the artist) leans into reality—the dirt and grime of survival, the sullen, grim folds of the psyche, the exquisite disappointments, the sour churn of rage, the smog of lust, the petty, uneven, disquieted moments that fall in between. The artist embraces ugliness and beauty with equal passion. The artist knows that this process is always, by its nature, inefficient. It is a slow effort without any promise of a concrete, external reward.

In order to create, the artist can't live behind walls or embrace fantasies. The artist must recognize that the real-world stakes are high, and control is hard to come by. The artist can't hide or sidestep total honesty or avoid taking a stand. How could the artist make something meaningful without revealing himself and his position in the world? He can't deny his emotions. He is forced to slow down and grapple with the injustices he encounters at every turn. To the committed artist, "extracting your max" sounds like yet another masturbatory pro tip, a way of turning inward as disappointments and upheaval threaten your good life.

In the introduction to *Tribe of Mentors,* Ferriss writes, "[S]uccess can usually be measured by the number of uncomfortable conversations we are willing to have, and by the number of uncomfortable actions we are willing to take." The guru's words sound so wise in a vacuum, or printed on a poster, or tapped out in a tweet. Yet Ferriss neglects to address the fact that it matters a great deal what *kinds* of conversations we have, what *kinds* of actions we take, and on whose behalf we act.

It makes perfect sense, really, that Ferriss begins his book

with this question: "What would this look like if it were easy?"
The point is not to dig into hard things. The point, always and
forever, is to clear an effortless path before you. You are to
avoid "unnecessary hardship," by asking abstract questions
like "[W]hat happens if we frame things in terms of elegance
instead of strain?"

Here's what happens: We elegantly proceed to publish sterile, platinum-elite "wisdom"-lite, assembled into a 589-page
tome that exists only within a hermetically sealed bubble of
the self. Such a book will be a comfort to your personal tribe of
fledgling, wannabe gurus, because their goals match yours: to
float high above the grime of life and the rage of injustice. The
aim is always to maximize your own gains while thoroughly
expunging the inconvenient humanity out of yourself. Ideally,
we will all evolve into disease-free, highly efficient, healthy,
joy-seeking low-body-fat robots, safe in our bunkers, free to
snack on cashew cheese and sulfate-free wine and peruse inspirational quotes as the world burns down outside our doors.

But the real moral of *Tribe of Mentors* lies elsewhere within
the book's pages: "Don't trust gurus, whether a marketing
guru or a life guru," writes entrepreneur-turned-philanthropist
Jérôme Jarre. "The guru separates himself from the rest of us.
Anything that creates separation is an illusion. In reality, we
are all united, all the same, all smart parts of the same bigger
thing, the universe."

Jarre then pinpoints the state of affairs that keeps the entire
guru industry afloat: "Most of the world is asleep today, playing a small role in a gigantic illusion. You don't have to be.
You can choose a different life. It's all within. You will know
the answers when you take the time to find yourself and trust
yourself." This message necessarily counters much of Ferriss's
offerings, since it entirely obviates the need for the products
he peddles so relentlessly. And not surprisingly, this message

alone upstages most of Ferriss's repetitive tome: You don't need more of anything to find your true path. You have everything you need already.

What Jarre implies but doesn't spell out is that this realization tends to transcend the self, building momentum until it becomes something much bigger and more expansive and porous. Because once we learn to cultivate compassion for ourselves *without* improvements or upgrades, we also learn to have compassion for other people, as broken and flawed and different from us as they might be. And if we're ever going to recognize that our survival is inextricably linked, this is how we're going to get there. We can no longer close the doors to the outside world and expect to survive. In fact, we have to resist the temptation to handle our fear by placing ourselves above others, or by building up our fortress walls. We are called to reject the "gigantic illusion" of our separateness and see reality clearly at last.

In other words, at this late date in human history, it would behoove most of us to think less like gurus and more like artists—deeply connected to ourselves and each other, painfully, beautifully aware of reality, and exquisitely alive to the moment—in order to build a new world outside of the toxic illusions of this one.

my mother's house

My mother's house has loud plumbing. There is a musty smell to most of its rooms. The screen doors don't close completely, leaving a crack where bugs can crawl in. In the summer, there are large flying insects waiting on the front door when you get home at night. The front yard is covered in clover but very little grass. The windows are big and the frames are rusted metal and hard to crank open.

My mother's house is not air-conditioned. She is one of the last humans alive in the swampy North Carolina heat without any relief beyond whirring fans. There are tiny spiders that live in the corners and no one kills them or cares that they've taken up residence there. There are windows with glass so old it looks a little warped. There are pine needles in the gutters. The shutters need painting. The bathroom could use a wastebasket.

In the bathroom cabinets, there are bandages and Epsom salts and weird brands of shampoo like Body On Tap that date back to 1987. When I visited a few months ago, I found a little jar of Vicks VapoRub that looked like it had been excavated from someone's garden sometime around 1975.

I grew up in that house. My mother sleeps in my bedroom now. The mini-blinds are still peach, the color I chose for the room, but the walls have been painted dark brown. The stairs are very steep. The ceilings are high. The chairs in the dining room have curved metal backs that dig into your shoulder blades. The table shakes when you touch it. The backyard is carpeted with pine needles, ornamented with ivy and pine trees. There is an old garage with a creaky door and a roof covered in leaves. My mother's car is twenty years old. My mother is seventy-five years old.

When I arrive at my mother's house in the summer, a cacophony of small creatures surrounds her house—birds singing, cicadas buzzing, tree frogs humming. Because there is no air-conditioning, you have to keep the windows open at night, which means yielding to this rain forest symphony. Sometimes there are crickets in the actual room with you. If you leave your phone on for a few too many minutes after you turn the lights out, tiny unidentified bugs will hit your phone screen repeatedly. You are never alone.

Pine trees tower over her house, a threat during big thunderstorms, which happen at least twice a week in the summer. The thunder is louder than any thunder you've ever heard, partly because the windows are open. You don't forget that her house is surrounded by tall trees, on a hill, when you hear that thunder. You remember the pine tree that was struck right outside the big dining room window. You remember how the whole world was just an orange and red flash. The tree splintered to bits. Weeks later, the bugs moved into it. My mother felt relieved that no one in the house was hurt. She said we had a lot to be grateful for.

And I do feel grateful every time I visit and a big storm rolls in. There is nothing like lying on that bad futon mattress on the floor of the den, listening to the thunder, watching the branches lash around in the wind, hearing the rain hammer the roof and the windows. You're inside but you feel like you're outside, as you wait for the storm to pass, as you wait for the cool breezes to arrive after the rain.

And in the morning, you hear the birds. The leaves of the trees dance in the dappled sunlight. The trees go on forever out there, straight into the sky. It's hard to get up off that hard futon when you can stare up at those trees from the floor, through windows six feet tall.

My mom and dad were going to rent the house at first. A professor and his German wife owned it, but then they decided to move back to D.C., because the German wife hated our small Southern town. My mother told my father, "We need to buy that house. That is a great house." My father found out the house was $24,000. My mother said to him, "That house is a steal. We have to buy it."

This was 1971. They bought the house. It was the best decision my mother ever made. Her marriage ended ten years later. My dad died fifteen years after that. There were disappointments and heartaches, but that house was never one of them. The cicadas and the birds and the little flying bugs and the crickets and the squirrels and the chipmunks and the tiny spiders and the mold and the rot and the creaky stairs and the thunderstorms all agree with her. That house never disappointed any of us.

Our visitors were always a little disappointed, though. They didn't appreciate the lack of air-conditioning, the bugs, the yapping dogs. How could they be so immune to its charms?

They probably lived in houses with double-paned windows, sealed off from the birds and the storms, sterile and quiet and dull. They probably closed their blinds at night and cranked up their buzzing central AC units. "You might as well sleep in the middle of a shopping mall," my mom often says.

When you leave my mother's house, it's true that you might feel *some* relief at the thought of returning to the comforts of modern life. But when you get back to your own house, your ordinary windows and doors that shut tightly will feel like a disappointment. Your dry California air and your swimming pool will feel like trifles compared to trees so tall they disappear into the sky. I used to think that my mother's house was embarrassing, a ramshackle mess in a small town, nothing and nowhere. Now I know that my mother's house is the center of the universe. There is no other place like it.

the miracle of the mundane

On a good day, all of humanity's accomplishments feel personal: the soaring violins of the second allegretto movement of Beethoven's Symphony no. 7, the intractable painted stare of Frida Kahlo, the enormous curving spans of the Golden Gate Bridge, the high wail of PJ Harvey's voice on "Victory," the last melancholy pages of Wallace Stegner's *Angle of Repose*. These works remind us that we're connected to the past and our lives have limitless potential. We were built to touch the divine.

On a bad day, all of humanity's failures feel unbearably personal: coyotes wandering city streets due to encroaching wildfires, American citizens in Puerto Rico enduring another day without electricity or potable water in the wake of Hurricane Maria, neo-Nazis spouting hatred in American towns, world leaders testing missiles that would bring the deaths of millions of innocent people. We encounter bad news in the intimate glow of our cell phone screens, and then project our worries onto the flawed artifacts of our broken world: the FOR LEASE sign on the upper level of the strip mall, the crow picking at a hamburger wrapper in the gutter, the pink stucco walls of the McMansion flanked by enormous square hedges, the blaring TVs on the walls of the local restaurant. On bad days, each moment is haunted by a palpable but private sense of dread. We feel irrelevant at best, damned at worst. Our only hope is to numb and distract ourselves as well as we can on our long, slow march to the grave.

On a good day, humankind's creations make us feel like we're here for a reason. Our belief sounds like the fourth molto allegro movement of Mozart's Symphony no. 41, *Jupiter:* Our hearts seem to sing along to Mozart's climbing strings, telling us that if we're patient, if we work hard, if we believe, if we stay focused, we will continue to feel joy, to do meaningful work, to show up for each other, to grow closer to some sacred ground. We are thrillingly alive and connected to every other living thing, in perfect, effortless accord with the natural world.

But it's hard to sustain that feeling, even on the best of days—to keep the faith, to stay focused on what matters most—because the world continues to besiege us with messages that we are failing. You're feeding your baby a bottle and a voice on the TV tells you that your hair should be shinier. You're reading a book but someone on Twitter wants you to know about a hateful thing a politician said earlier this morning. You are bedraggled and inadequate and running late for something and it's always this way. You are busy and distracted. You are not here.

It's even worse on a bad day, when humankind's creations

fill us with the sense that we are failing as a people, as a planet, and nothing can be done about it. The chafing smooth jazz piped into the immaculate coffee joint, the fake cracks painted on the wall at the Cheesecake Factory, the smoke from fires burning thousands of acres of dry tinder, blotting out the sun— they remind us that even though our planet is in peril, we are still being teased and flattered into buying stuff that we don't need, or coaxed into forgetting the truth about our darkening reality. As the crowd around us watches a fountain dance to Frank Sinatra's "Somewhere Beyond the Sea" at the outdoor mall, we peek at our phones and discover the bellowed warnings of an erratic foreign leader, threatening to destroy us from thousands of miles away. Everything cheerful seems to have an ominous shadow looming behind it now. The smallest images and bits of news can feel so invasive, so frightening. They erode our belief in what the world can and should be.

As the first total solar eclipse in America in thirty-nine years reveals itself, an email lands in my inbox from ABC that says THE GREAT AMERICAN ECLIPSE at the top. People are tweeting and retweeting the same eclipse jokes all morning. As the day grows dimmer, I remember that Bonnie Tyler is going to sing her 1983 hit "Total Eclipse of the Heart" on an eclipse-themed cruise off the coast of Florida soon.

Even natural wonders aren't what they used to be, because nothing can be experienced without commentary. In the 1950s, we worried about how TV would affect our culture. Now our entire lives are a terrible talk show that we can't turn off. It often feels like we're struggling to find ourselves and each other in a crowded, noisy room. We are plagued, around the clock, by the shouting and confusion and fake intimacy of the global community, mid–nervous breakdown.

Sometimes it feels like our shared breakdown is making us less generous and less focused. On a bad day, the world seems

to be filled with bad books and bad buildings and bad songs
and bad choices. Worthwhile creations and ego-driven, sloppy
works are treated to the same hype and praise; soon it starts
to feel as if everything we encounter was designed merely to
make some carefully branded human a fortune. Why aren't
we reaching for more than this? Isn't art supposed to inspire or
provoke or make people feel emotions that they don't necessarily *want* to feel? Can't the moon block out the sun without a
1980s pop accompaniment? So much of what is created today
seems engineered to numb or distract us, keeping us dependent
on empty fixes indefinitely.

Such creations feel less like an attempt to capture the divine
than a precocious student's term paper. If any generous spirit
shines through, it's manufactured in the hopes of a signal
boost, so that some leisure class end point can be achieved. Our
world is glutted with products that exist to help someone seize
control of their own life while the rest of the globe falls to ruin.
Work (and guidance, and leadership) that comes from such a
greedy, uncertain place has more in common with that fountain at the outdoor mall, playing the same songs over and over,
every note an imitation of a note played years before.

But human beings are not stupid. We can detect muddled
and self-serving intentions in the artifacts we encounter. Even
so, such works slowly infect us with their lopsided values.
Eventually, we can't help but imagine that this is the only way
to proceed: by peddling your own wares at the expense of the
wider world. Can't we do better than this, reach for more, *insist*
on more? Why does our culture make us feel crazy for trying?

———

Mozart composed an enormous volume of music over the
course of his short life, working relentlessly from his youth to

his death. He composed music as a child in a horse-drawn carriage, traveling with his father. He wrote music even when he was very sick or in debt. And though he is often portrayed as temperamental, unsteady, and erratic, his productivity never suffered. He found a way to shut out distractions and do the hard, patient work necessary to compose transcendent music.

Mozart's father, Leopold, viewed his son's musical talent as a miracle given by God. He believed that it was his job to help Mozart share his miracle with the world. In Mozart's time, composers weren't seen as an exalted class of humans. As Paul Johnson writes in his biography of Mozart, "Musicians were exactly in the same position as other household servants—cooks, chambermaids, coachmen, and sentries. They existed for the comfort and well-being of their masters and mistresses." Leopold Mozart didn't agree. He believed "that his son should be displayed 'to the glory of God,' as he put it."

Imagine being told that your talent is a miracle, and you have just one job. You don't have to be happy or successful or attractive or well-balanced as a human being. You don't have to accrue wealth or maintain lots of friendships or seem impressive in any other way. You don't have to tweet or share photos of your latest sheet music on Instagram or start a podcast about composing to increase your visibility and expand the size of your platform. You just have to do your one job to the best of your ability. Imagine being told that you have been given your talent by God, and you must honor God's will by manifesting that talent in your creations.

This would likely come as an enormous relief to many of us, the same way that witnessing a total eclipse all by yourself, in an empty field with no Wi-Fi, sounds like an impossible luxury. Working in a small, dark room, alone—it almost sounds thrilling next to a life jacked into the nonstop, infinite chattering matrix.

Living simply today takes work. It takes work to overcome the noise that has accumulated in our heads, growing louder and more pervasive since we were young. It takes work to overcome the illusion that we will arrive at some end point where we will be better—more successful, adored, satisfied, relaxed, rich. It takes hard work to say, "This is how I am," in a calm voice, without anxiously addressing how you should be. It takes work to shift your focus from the smudges on the window to the view outside. It requires conscious effort not to waste your life swimming furiously against the tide, toward some imaginary future that will never make you happy anyway.

Even once you accept that you're just another regular mortal and not some supernatural force who deserves to live like a king—a message encoded in the background noise of our daily lives, rich, poor, or somewhere in the insecure in-between—it's still hard not to wish for something more exciting than calm acceptance. It's hard not to wish for the romance of movies, the soul-bearing friendships of books, the egalitarian ideals of Martin Luther King, Jr., the miraculous talent of Mozart.

Today Mozart might be seen as an outcast: His behavior was often impulsive, he made up his own mind about his compositions, he thought nothing of thwarting convention, he rarely had enough money, he died young. But when you listen to his music, it's impossible not to believe that he was a joyful and deeply satisfied human being. Johnson backs this up: Mozart was so certain of his one job and his ability to do it that he didn't care at all about how he looked, how he sounded, how he seemed. He treated his talent like it was a miracle.

And maybe when he died, he didn't think, "Is this all I get?" the way we, the narrow-minded living, might imagine, in the face of such a premature death. Maybe he thought, "I lived a rich life. I embraced what I was given, and it was incredible."

Many of us learn to construct a clear and precise vision of

what we want, but we're never taught how to enjoy what we actually have. There will always be more victories to strive for, more strangers to charm, more images to collect and pin to our vision boards. It's hard to want what we have; it's far easier to want everything in the world. So this is how we live today: by stuffing ourselves to the gills, yet somehow it only makes us more anxious, more confused, and more hungry. We are hurtling forward—frantic, dissatisfied, and perpetually lost.

Our bewildered state doesn't just injure us individually; it impedes our ability to work together for a better world. We can't stand for justice and effect change until we've learned to push away empty temptations, shiny dead ends, and trivial distractions. As long as we're perpetually assaulted by a barrage of news and tweets and texts, as long as commercial messages and smooth brands and profit-minded discourse are our only relief from our insecure realities, we'll never develop the ability to live in the present moment. We have to cultivate compassion for ourselves and each other. We have to connect with each other in genuine and meaningful ways. But we also have to relearn how to breathe in the late summer air and feel the sunshine, to admire the swelling pink clouds and shut out the hiss of truck brakes, to sit on the ground and look up at the trees without looking ahead to what we'll post on Facebook about it. You can have your eclipse and I will have mine. You can call yours a miracle and I will call mine a certain slant of light, like the one Emily Dickinson described: heavenly and oppressive and fleeting.

—

There's a scene in Elif Batuman's *The Idiot* in which our protagonist, Selin, who is a student at Harvard, goes to see a therapist. After Selin explains that she feels alienated from her fellow students, her teachers, and herself, her therapist replies, "I'm interested in your comment that most people are 'so awful.' What makes most people awful?"

Selin tells him that most people, the second they meet you, are sizing you up as competition for the same resources. "It was as if everyone lived in fear of a shipwreck, where only so many people would fit on the lifeboat, and they were constantly trying to stake out their property and identify the dispensable people—people they could get rid of."

"Do you see yourself as one of the dispensable people?" the therapist asks. Selin replies, "The point is, I don't want to get involved in that question, and it's all most people want to talk about." She explains that not many people seem interested in "what you're like." They just want to figure out what you're worth.

Instead of recognizing that what Selin wants from the world is a divine and magical kind of connection between disparate souls, the therapist reveals himself to be precisely the kind of sorter Selin has described. He assumes that she is mostly consumed by a "fear of competition and a fear of rejection by [her] peers." She is focused on success and fears failure, and she's suffering from the low self-esteem common to all of the ultra-competitive students at Harvard. "You rationalize the rejection of your peers by telling yourself it comes from other people's deficiencies rather than your own. *They* can't understand your philosophy or your ideas."

The therapist's misinterpretation of Selin's problems presents one of the most succinct and terrifying summaries of our current delusions that I've found anywhere. We are encouraged to believe in our dreams, but we are assumed to dream in the same limited palette as everyone else. We are to view ourselves as unique snowflakes only as it facilitates more efficiently melting ourselves into bottled spring water. Our ultimate value is always quantifiable. All magic is lost to our sad economies of survival. Competition always supersedes connection.

The therapist tries to soothe Selin by reassuring her that *she will win eventually*. This flavor of "sensitivity" ends up sounding more like a commercial for laundry detergent or a movie about superheroes: Selin is worthy, she is in the fight, she might yet remain on the boat with the survivors. There is no acknowledgment that the game is rigged, and that even if, by some small chance, she does "win" (however dispensables or indispensables might define winning), it's unlikely to bring her satisfaction so much as even more anxiety and fear and alienation. Instead of treating her sensitive observation of her fellow students' scarcity mentality as the miracle that it is, the therapist pathologizes her gift of sight. Selin has dared to be completely honest, only to encounter yet another human being who can't place her outside of her position in a tireless race to the top.

Selin wants more than the hopelessly mundane acquaintanceships that everyone around her seems to accept. She's been corresponding online with a fellow student named Ivan whom she knows in real life, though they rarely talk. But in their letters to each other, which are so abstract and odd and lovely that they're sometimes difficult to grasp, they attempt some form of mutual understanding, but achieve something even more powerful and important: a way of daring to be bigger and more brilliant than their circumstances and their peers in real life will allow. By celebrating their individual peculiarities and fears and odd perspectives honestly, they begin to experience each other's strange, narrow views—and flaws and shortcomings—as engrossing and important and even boundless. They treat each other the way Mozart's father treated him. They say to each other, "Whatever is here, even when it feels a little dark, even when it confuses me, I have chosen to view it as divine." Their connection is a kind of a miracle, against a landscape dominated by people more like the therapist—people with good intentions who nonetheless tell stories that lead in circles, further and further away from the truth.

If we didn't succumb to our culture's perplexing, destructive messages, something might shift. We might find ways to support each other more radically, more selflessly, without distractions, without anticipating a celebratory end point: *That* might allow us to generate the kind of beauty and connection and honesty that Dickinson and Mozart and Stegner brought us, the kind of blazing majesty that burns through the confusion and bewilderment, that feels intimate and personal, that lights up each new moment with endless possibility.

—

We are living in a time of extreme delusion, disorientation, and dishonesty. At this unparalleled moment of self-consciousness and self-loathing, commercial messages have replaced real connection or faith as our guiding religion. These messages depend on convincing us that we don't have enough yet, and that everything valuable and extraordinary exists outside of ourselves.

It's not surprising that in a culture dominated by such messages, many people believe that humility will only lead to being crushed under the wheels of capitalism or subsumed by some malevolent force that abhors weakness. Our anxious age erodes our ability to be open and show our hearts to each other. It severs our ability to connect to the purity and magic that we carry around inside us already, without anything to buy, without anything new to become, without any way to conquer and win the shiny luxurious lives we're told we deserve. So instead of passionately embracing the things we love the most, and in so doing reveal our fragility and self-hatred and sweetness and darkness and fear and everything that makes us whole, we present a fractured, tough, protected self to the world. Our shiny robot soldiers do battle with other shiny robot soldiers, each side calling the other side "terrible," because in a world that can't see poetry or recognize the divinity of each living soul, fragility curdles into macho toughness and soulless rage. All nuance is lost in a fearful rush to turn every passing thought or idea or belief into dogma.

Against this landscape, anything that celebrates the wildness and complexity of the human soul is worthy of celebration. This is true in a global sense, in communities, and it's true within a single human being. The antidote to a world that tells us sick stories about ourselves and poisons us into thinking that we're helpless is believing in our world and in our communities and in ourselves.

We must reconnect with what it means to be human: fragile, intensely fallible, and constantly humbled. We must believe in and embrace the conflicted nature of humankind. That means that even as we stop trying to live our imaginary, glorious "best lives," we still have the audacity to believe in our own brilliance and talent and vision—even if that sometimes sounds grandiose, delusional, or unjust. We have to embrace what we already have and be who we already are, but we also have to honor the intensity and romance and longing that batter around inside of our heads and our hearts. We have to honor the richness of our inner lives and the inherent values that are embedded there.

But we should also aim to create a self and a life and an artistic vision that aren't an escape from ordinary life, but a way of rendering ordinary life for people of every color, shape, size, and background more magical *to them*. In order to do that, we have to see that every human is divine. We have to train ourselves to see that with our own eyes. It will fuel us, once we see it. The ordinary people around us, the angry ones and the indifferent ones, the good ones and the bad ones, will start to glow and shimmer.

It's important to recognize that even in the most compromised-seeming relationships and situations, even in the most imperfect life circumstances, you can find sustenance and grace. Even when you feel polluted by a repetitive, aggressive world and alienated from the people within it, if you look closer there is something real and beautiful there, some attempt to feel, to connect, to improve the world we have.

Did Mozart truly believe that his musical gifts were a miracle? Perhaps he simply resolved to believe in them the way his father did. That's the kind of faith we require: We have to believe each and every day, in spite of a steady onslaught of setbacks and discouragement. We have to believe in our gifts. We have to believe in our peculiarities and our flaws. We have to believe in our capacity to love. We have to believe that what we do and how we live matters, like a once-in-four-decades phenomenon, like a miracle.

We have to recognize that when we feel conflicted and sick about our place in the world, that's often true because our world was built to sell us things and to make us feel inadequate and needy. As the art critic John Berger puts it, in *Ways of Seeing*:

It is necessary to make an imaginative effort which runs contrary to the whole contemporary trend of the art world: it is necessary to see works of art freed from all the mystique which is attached to them as property objects. It then becomes possible to see them as testimony to the process of their own making instead of as products; to see them in terms of action instead of finished achievement. The question: what went into the making of this? supersedes the collector's question of: what is this?

We are called to resist viewing ourselves as consumers or as commodities. We are called to savor the process of our own slow, patient development, instead of suffering in an enervated, anxious state over our value and our popularity. We are called to view our actions as important, with or without consecration by forces beyond our control. We are called to plant these seeds in our world: to dare to tell every living soul that they already matter, that their seemingly mundane lives are a slowly unfolding mystery, that their small choices and acts of generosity are vitally important.

Here is how you will start: You will recognize that you are not headed for some imaginary finish line, some state of "best"ness that will finally bring you peace. You will see that you are as much of a miracle as Mozart was. You will remember that bit of advice lurking inside one of Shirley Jackson's dark novels: "Somewhere, deep inside you, hidden by all sorts of fears and worries and petty little thoughts, is a clean pure being made of radiant colors." You will feel this and know it in your heart and pass this feeling along to the people around you. You will breathe in this moment—this imperfect, uncertain, not-quite-right, heavenly moment.

You will say to yourself, "It is enough." And it will be.

acknowledgments

I want to thank my editor, Yaniv Soha, for encouraging all of my absurd whims and then patiently making my words a million times better. I'd also like to thank Bill Thomas and everyone else at Doubleday for being kind and enthusiastic and supportive. Michael Goldsmith in particular is the best publicist in the world, sharp and savvy and calm under pressure. I would like to be more like him.

I'd like to thank my agent, Sarah Burnes, who is always soothing but fights hard when she needs to. And thank you to Brooke Ehrlich, who makes Hollywood seem like just another nice place to eat lunch with some smart people. Big thanks to my brilliant boss at *New York* magazine, Stella Bugbee, along with my smart, generous editors Molly Fischer and Jen Gann.

Thank you to Kelly Atkins, Apryl Lundsten, Meghan Daum,

Perri Kersh, Carter Kersh, Andrea Russell, Lisa Glatt, David Hernandez, Jillian Lauren, Chantel Cappiello, Ken Basart, Carina Chocano, Ken Layne, and Jason Berlin for your enthusiasm, loyalty, and seriously weird ways. I love you guys.

Thanks to my mom, Susan Havrilesky, who can always squeeze a little joy and excitement from whatever she has on hand. Thanks to Eric Havrilesky, Laura Havrilesky, Melissa Hernandez, and Jeff Welch. Thanks to my favorite nephew Calvin and my other favorite nephew Eli and my other favorite nephews Alex and Marsden, and thank you to Nicola, my favorite niece of all. Thank you to Uncle Roger for teaching us all about staying calm and cheerful under duress, and thank you to Aunt Jean and Aunt Hilda for making our beach trip my favorite vacation every year. Thank you to my husband, Bill Sandoval, who makes every single day better. And a giant thank you to Zeke, Claire, and Ivy, three wild freaks with big hearts. I am very lucky to know you.

about the author

Heather Havrilesky is the author of *How to Be a Person in the World* and the memoir *Disaster Preparedness*. She is a columnist for *New York* magazine, and has written for *The New Yorker*, *The Atlantic*, *The New York Times Magazine*, and NPR's *All Things Considered*, among others. She was *Salon*'s TV critic for seven years. She lives in Los Angeles with her husband and a loud assortment of dependents, most of them nondeductible.

what if this were enough?